DONKEY BUSINESS

COMMERCE WITH A PURPOSE

BY PETER J. BRISCOE

COMPASS
-finances God's way ™

CONTENTS

ABOUT THE AUTHOR

Peter Briscoe an Englishman, born in 1950, studied Industrial Chemistry and Management at Loughborough University of Technology. He moved to The Netherlands in 1974 and was asked by his company to set up a subsidiary in Holland, selling chemical specialties to the aerospace and food processing industries. From 1986 to 2002, Peter was Executive Director of CBMC, Christian Businessmen's Committees, in Holland.

In 1990, Peter set up "Synthesys". a consulting company specializing in chemical product development. When the Berlin Wall collapsed in 1990, Peter developed Europartners, a movement dedicated to reaching European business and professional leaders for Christ.

From 2002, Peter took an assignment as Managing Director of HE Space Operations, serving the European Space institutions, specializing in providing professional services for spaceflight activities.

From 2008, Peter retired from business to develop a movement of Biblical stewardship in Europe, first of all through Crown Financial Ministries and then Compass - finances God's way.

At home, Peter is Chair of the Church board of the Baptist Church of Leiden. He is married to his Dutch wife, Didie since 1972. They have three daughters and six grandchildren.

ABOUT THE BOOK

Donkey Business is a challenge to Christians in business to look at their business in a different way.

God has not only called us to share our faith on Sunday with our fellow believers, but especially with those whom we meet in the dark depths of the business jungle, where we are sent out as "sheep amidst the wolves."

Many people think that being a Christian and doing business are two different worlds. Christian businessmen are often accused of being holy on Sunday and not wholly true the rest of the week.

In this book, Peter Briscoe helps connect our Christian walk with the daily challenges of business. The donkey is a metaphor for an enterprise and the book explains how the donkey, the business can be used by God to bear fruit in the marketplace.

DEDICATION

To a few entrepreneurs who have helped me to understand the meaning of doing business with God:

Al Diepeveen of Kankakee, Illinois, who taught me, "You can't out-give God!"

Kent Humphreys of Oklahoma City, Oklahoma, who taught me, "Your business is your ministry."

Jim Johnston of Belfast, Northern Ireland, who taught me, "The best thing you can do for anyone is to set them free!"

Gunnar Olson of Orebro, Sweden, who first challenged me to do a Bible study on donkeys and set me off on the road to Donkey Business;

And to my beloved wife, Didie, thank you for putting up with this silly ass for more than forty-five years!

FOREWORD TO THE 1ST EDITION

You are about to begin a great adventure. If you are an entrepreneur like me, then you are going to love Donkey Business, Commerce with a Purpose. There are hundreds of books coming out every year in this massive move of God in the marketplace. However, few of them are as much fun and informative as this book. I have enjoyed business for the last forty years and consider myself a student of God's Word. So, if you are like me and are serious about business and your walk with God, then you are going to really enjoy this journey.

I had always considered donkeys kind of plain and not very glamorous. I had no idea that I could learn so much from a donkey about my business. Peter Briscoe does a wonderful job of using the metaphor of the donkey to share the hidden secrets from God's Word that every business leader needs to learn.

For several years now, I have led an organization of Christian CEO's and business owners. I have come to realize that each of these leaders faces similar challenges to the ones that I experience in the businesses in which I am still involved. Peter uses his years of experience in business and his knowledge of God's Word to address many of these issues that you and I face every day in our professions. His personal examples and practical suggestions will be extremely helpful for every business leader who wants to avoid the pitfalls of the painful detours on our marketplace journey. He shows us how we need to establish a constant connection to Jesus Christ, who will guide us through the difficult decisions of leading a business.

Peter Briscoe is the perfect leader to share these principles with us. He has a proven track record as a leader in industry. Peter is one most respected Christian business leaders in Europe and has earned this by years of leading in business while walking with Christ. I have had the pleasure of knowing Peter and working with him for some years now and believe that he is one of God's chosen messengers for us in the workplace. He has modeled these truths in his marriage, family, relationships, and profession. So, buckle up for the journey and listen closely as Peter shares with us the secrets of the donkey which is tied to the Vine.

Foreword to the first edition, April 2008.

Kent Humphreys, President
FCCI - Fellowship of Companies for Christ
(1946-2013)

FOREWORD TO THE 2ND EDITION

It is always a privilege to write a Foreword to a great book, but when that book is written by a true friend, then it is a double privilege!

I have known Peter for almost 20 years and have had the opportunity to work alongside him for 7 years. Peter Briscoe is an insightful man of God, a businessman who loves studying the Bible. He has a unique skill of being able to see within God's Word, specific principles relating to business. Donkey Business is one of these unique insights!

Within the pages of this book are timeless principles from many parts of the Bible that relate to business purpose, leadership and operations. You will find yourself being encouraged as a leader but also challenged to treasure God's Word more, as a source of your own business wisdom!

Peter takes us on an intellectual and spiritual journey that is sure to challenge and change the way we view business and its effect on us and the people our business influences. As you read deeper and deeper into the book you will see why I was so thrilled to be under the influence of this Godly man!

J. David Rae
Former President Apple Canada
September 2018.

DONKEY POEM

When fishes flew and forests walked

  And figs grew upon a thorn,

Some moment when the moon was blood

  Then surely I was born.

With monstrous head and sickening cry

  And ears like errant wings,

The devils walking parody

  On all four-footed things.

The tattered outlaw of the earth,

  Of ancient crooked will;

Starve, scourge, and deride me: I am dumb,

  I keep my secret still.

Fools! For I also had my hour;

  One far fierce hour and sweet:

There was a shout about my ears,

  And palms before my feet.

—*G. K. Chesterton*

CALLED TO THE MARKETPLACE

Saul's Donkey Business

In the Bible we read how a talented young man, destined to become a great leader, was struggling with his calling and his business. Saul was the son of a wealthy businessman named Kish. Chapters 9 and 10 of First Samuel tell us that Saul was literally doing "donkey business"—looking after his family's donkeys—when God chose him to become king of Israel.

Kish's family business was in turmoil because some donkeys were lost. What was the matter? Had they been stolen by a competitor? Kish asked his son Saul, "an impressive young man without equal among the Israelites—a head taller than any of the others" (1 Sam. 9:2), to take a trustworthy co-worker with him to search for the lost animals. The company could not afford to lose such a valuable capital investment.

They traveled the country but could not find a trace of the donkeys. Saul was at his wits' end and said, "Come, let's go back, or my father will stop thinking about the donkeys and start worrying about us" (verse 5).

His assistant knew about a wise old man named Samuel who lived in a nearby town and, being a prophet, received special insight from God. Maybe he knew how to solve this problem. Surprisingly, Samuel was already waiting for them. The day before, God had told Samuel that a young man named Saul would visit him. Samuel even had a dinner party arranged. Thirty prominent guests were invited, and Saul was to be the guest of honor!

Saul didn't know what was happening to him. Those troublesome donkeys had brought him here, and now he wanted to go home as soon as possible. But after dinner, Samuel took him to another room and said, "God has anointed you to become king of Israel." Saul went on a business trip to look for the animals, but his search ended with the message that he would become king of Israel!

Saul, however, was not interested in that job at all. Samuel told him he would receive three signs so he would know that the assignment came from God, and then he sent Saul on his way. And all these three signs came to pass.

The first sign was that he did not have to worry about his personal and business matters. The donkeys had been found, his father no longer worried about them, and he wanted his son back in the office as soon as possible.

The second sign was that on his way back home, he would meet three men traveling to Bethel to worship God. They would ask about his welfare and give him what he needed for his daily sustenance.

And the last sign would be meeting a group of prophets at the Philistine guard post at Gibeon-Elohim coming down from their place of sacrifice, all in ecstasy. Musicians playing harps, tambourines, flutes, and lyres would precede the group of prophets. This meeting would result in Saul also being ecstatically gripped by the Holy Spirit and becoming a different person.

Saul turned around to leave Samuel and God "changed Saul's heart" (1 Sam. 10:9).

The people had difficulty believing the changes to Saul were real, and they asked themselves, "Whatever happened to Kish's son?"

What an experience for Saul—called from his donkey business to serve the Lord as king!

On his return home, Saul's uncle asked for a report of his business trip. You would think that Saul would be overflowing with enthusiasm about his conversion and the miracle that happened to him, but Saul reacted just like the businessman he was: "We went to look for the donkeys," he replied, "but we could not find them, so we went to Samuel."

"Well, what did he tell you?" asked Saul's uncle.

"He told us that the donkeys had been found," Saul replied, but he did not tell his uncle what Samuel had told him about becoming king. Not even a word! Saul kept his business to himself and had no interest in what God wanted with him, unless he could let God do what he wanted for himself. It very much looked like Saul did not want to accept his new assignment from God; he wanted to stay a businessman. But Samuel had not in the least finished with Saul. He told the people of Israel, "God has heard your request, and he will give you a king!"

Then Samuel gathered all the people of Israel and said to them, "Present yourselves before the Lord by your tribes and clans." (1 Sam. 10:19). When they did so, God chose first Saul's tribe, then his clan, then his family. Eventually, Saul was publicly chosen as king. The people went to look for him, but they could not find him. Then they asked the Lord, "Where is the missing person?" "He is there," the Lord said. "He is hiding among the baggage!"

Why did he hide himself? Was he shy, modest, or humble? No, he crept away because he wanted to live his life in his way. He tried to ignore God's calling. He preferred to stay with the donkeys and their precious load. Material things were more important to him than his mission.

My calling

I strongly believe that if you are in business and a Christian, then your business or your work constitutes a call from God to represent His interests in the marketplace you are involved in, as you go about your work. "Work willingly at whatever you do, as though you were working for the Lord rather than for people." (Colossians 3:23 nlt).

God still reaches out to us in the middle of our daily business transactions with new assignments!

I vividly remember my calling. When setting out on my career, I had created the goal of becoming managing director of a chemical company before I was thirty. I achieved that goal at the age of twenty-eight and was the managing director of a chemical company in the Netherlands, a subsidiary of a larger British public company. It was 1981 and we had experienced tough times in the business because of high inflation, scarce raw materials supply due to the squeezing of oil in the Middle East, and high interest rates. Still, our business was doing reasonably well. We had received large contracts from two flagship customers— KLM and the Royal Dutch Air Force—for the maintenance of airframes and turbine engines, and we were also able to take over a company that opened the door into a new market area, allowing us to sell many products to the lively nuclear energy market. Personally, however, this success came at a price. I paid heavily in three different areas.

The first was my health. Besides the burden of stress, physical problems due to carrying heavy drums of chemicals gave me a back hernia, and I had to go through surgery. During my stay in the hospital, I gave proxy to our accountant, who misused his mandate to steal funds from the business. This brought further financial burden on the business.

The second area was my family life. My wife had given birth to our third daughter via a caesarean section, and it was tough for her to be at home all day with three small children, with her husband working long hours and not paying attention to the family's needs. In those days, I put my work and my own needs at the top of my priority list, and my marriage and family life suffered as a result.

Third, my relationship with God took a hard hit at this busy time of my life. I had been an active Christian, involved in church life, but now I was no longer serving in that capacity. I had neither the time nor the energy at the end of a long, hard workday to spend time studying the Bible, praying, or serving at my church. I remember sitting in church one Sunday morning, and all I could think about was how to pay the bills the next day!

At that time, I was burdened down by the cares of managing a business, but God caught my attention! I remember sitting in my office, my heart heavy, and wondering what kind of man I had become. Looking back, I concluded that I was a success in business, but a failure in life!

I knew my existence didn't reflect who I wanted to be: a successful businessman, enjoying life and serving God. My mind drifted back to a special event in my life.

Five years before, my wife and I had attended a conference in Essen, Germany, organized by the Navigators, an interdenominational Christian movement, with whom I'd been associated since my university days. The conference theme was "Making Disciples in All Nations" in answer to Jesus' commission for us from Matthew 28:18–20, often called the Great Commission. We wanted to respond, so my wife and I committed ourselves that evening to fulfilling Jesus' calling in whatever way he wanted us to. However, five years later, this Great Commission had become for me the Great Omission! I had neglected the call and become buried in business.

Around that time, I met some Christian businessmen from CBMC, Christian Business Men's Committee, who invited me to join a small group meeting at seven o'clock each morning to discover what God had to say in the Bible about doing business and to pray together for our business and personal needs. These men helped me to sort out my priorities—to put God first, my wife and family second, and work last. I began to help other businesspeople who were in a position similar to mine: busy, tired, despondent, and unfulfilled.

After my original call back in 1977, I, just like Saul, had become busy with my "donkey business." It took me five years to respond to

God's attempts to get my attention. It seemed as if my business were speaking to me: "Peter, what are you risking for all this success? Is it worth it?"

Maybe you are concerned about what is happening to your business. Could this be God's way of getting your attention? Changes in circumstances are God's invitation to allow Him to speak to you and experience His guidance. In the following chapters, we will look at the donkey as a metaphor for business and consider the biblical account of a real donkey speaking to a businessman! Will you allow God to speak to you through your company?

To experience God's donkey business, first your donkey has to be led to the right place!

During a trip to Egypt, I heard the following story: Sammy had lost his donkey. He fell to his knees and thanked God. Ali watched in disbelief. "You lost your donkey," he said. "Why are you so thankful to God?" Sammy replied, "I thanked God he made sure I was not on that donkey at that time. Otherwise I would have been lost too!"

There's no need for you or your business to be lost, without direction. God wants to speak to you through your business. Read on to learn just what he has to say.

A DONKEY AS A METAPHOR FOR A BUSINESS

2

A farmer's donkey died. The farmer really needed a donkey to do all sorts of necessary jobs at the farm, so he called a local donkey dealer.

This man had a donkey for sale for $1000. The farmer agreed to transfer the money, and the dealer promised to deliver the donkey as soon as possible. But when the trailer arrived a week later, the donkey in it was dead.

The farmer phoned the trader and said, "Hey, the donkey you sold me was dead on arrival!"

"That's too bad. What are we going to do now?"

"You'll have to get me another donkey," said the farmer. "I'm sorry, but that was my last one."

"Well now, if you can't get me another, you'd better send my money back."

"Unfortunately, that's not possible. I've already spent it. "Never mind, then," said the farmer. "I'll just raffle off the donkey."

"Raffle off a dead donkey? You can't do that!" "Sure I can."

A few weeks later the trader called back, curious to know the outcome of the ridiculous raffle.

"It all went very well," the farmer said. "I sold five hundred raffle tickets for two dollars each and made a tidy profit."

The trader was shocked and asked, "Weren't the people very angry when they found out that the donkey was dead?"

"Oh no, only the man who won the donkey," the farmer replied. "So I give him his two dollars back!"

Donkeys in the Old Testament

The most common word used for a donkey, or ass, in the Old Testament is '*chamor*,' which, according to the International Standard Bible Encyclopedia, likely includes the idea of carrying a burden. Donkeys were employed in the caravans of commerce and sent even on long expeditions through the desert. '*Chamor*' also represents physical, material possessions that we use to serve us. Adam looked into the face of each of the animals he was to name and called the donkey '*chamor*', an animal that carries heavy, physical burdens and is destined to serve man's purposes.

In Old Testament times, donkeys were a special indication of wealth. It is said about Jacob that he "grew exceedingly prosperous and came to own large flocks, and maidservants and menservants, and camels and donkeys" (Gen. 30:43).

Donkeys were not only an indication of wealth, but also an indispensable means of conducting business. Joseph sent to his father, Jacob, "ten donkeys loaded with the best things of Egypt, and ten female donkeys loaded with grain and bread and other provisions for his journey" (Gen. 45:23).

A donkey was also the preferred means of transport for highly placed citizens. When David had gone a little beyond the summit of the Mount of Olives, Ziba, the servant of Mephibosheth, was waiting there for him. He had two donkeys loaded with 200 loaves of bread, 100 clusters of raisins, 100 bunches of summer fruit, and a wineskin full of wine. "What are these for?" the king asked Ziba. Ziba replied,

"The donkeys are for the king's people to ride on, and the bread and summer fruit are for the young men to eat. The wine is for those who become exhausted in the wilderness." (2 Sam. 16:1–2 nlt)

The prophet Isaiah described entrepreneurs carrying their assets on donkey's backs, throughout a jungle of a marketplace filled with risk on every side and yielding little profit at the end: "The caravan moves slowly across the terrible desert to Egypt—donkeys weighed down with riches and camels loaded with treasure—all to pay for Egypt's protection. They travel through the wilderness, a place of lionesses and lions, a place where vipers and poisonous snakes live. All this, and Egypt will give you nothing in return" (Isa. 30:6 nlt).

The Metaphorical Donkey

I like to think that the donkey is a biblical metaphor for a business. Your business is a vehicle to carry your load, a means to use to reach your goal and to achieve your purposes, something that comprises your assets or wealth.

The marketplace is not necessarily friendly toward a Christian businessperson. Doing business brings about misery when you reach your credit limit and creditors threaten with bankruptcy; you experience hardship when your biggest customer cancels an important order, and when the economy falls more sharply than a barometer during a storm. You encounter lions in the form of roaring competitors who threaten to swallow you up, cunning snakes in the shape of an opponent who does not value the truth, yes, even vipers as quick as lightning in the shape of hostile takeovers or forced negotiations. It is not surprising that an entrepreneur will ask him- or herself, "Why am I doing this? It seems I'm losing as fast as I'm gaining!"

Some years ago, I was CEO of a company specializing in human spaceflight services. Our offices were close to the technical center of ESA, the European Space Agency, in the Netherlands. As a government agency funded by the member states of the European

Union, contracts granted for technical and engineering support had to be re-competed every few years. It happened that at this time, 80 percent of our contracts with ESA were all up for renewal. Now, these were lucrative five-year contracts for specialized personnel to manage projects to support operations on the International Space Station. You can imagine that our competitors wanted to muscle in on the business, and in the period of preparing our proposals for the new contracts, they certainly flexed their muscles in an attempt to edge us out. We were the largest single supplier and, of course, the best!

This created a kind of free-for-all feeding frenzy, as our competitors realized how large the contracts were and that they were all up for grabs! They offered our key personnel huge, disproportionate salaries to jump ship and join the competition. That, along with the use of several other dirty tricks, made it tough for us to keep faith that God would continue to provide for us as he always had done in the past. We determined not to compromise our ethics and to remain true to God in the face of ferocious competition.

When the dust settled, we came through well, the continuity of the business was secured, and I could go on to another assignment.

Today, as Christian businesspeople, we experience the reality of a demanding and capricious business climate. There are plenty of reasons to ask ourselves, "Why am I doing all this?" or even, "Is this all there is?"

But, there is good news! The prophet Zechariah wrote, "Rejoice, O people of Zion! Shout in triumph, O people of Jerusalem! Look, your king is coming to you. He is righteous and victorious, yet he is humble, riding on a donkey—riding on a donkey's colt. I will remove the battle chariots from Israel and the war- horses from Jerusalem. I will destroy all the weapons used in battle, and your king will bring peace to the nations." (Zech. 9:9–10 nlt)

This prophecy was fulfilled when Jesus rode into Jerusalem on a donkey on what we now call Palm Sunday in preparation for the week ahead, which led to his crucifixion. (Incidentally, a donkey has a dark stripe across his shoulders and a stripe across his backbone, thereby forming a cross!) Jesus used a donkey to achieve his purpose, and I believe he wants to use your donkey, your business or your company, to accomplish his work in the world today.

Some years ago, I started a group of Christian entrepreneurs, which we called, "Crown Companies." A Crown company is essentially a business whose CEO is Jesus Christ, and is completely devoted to his goals. We wanted to see Jesus 'ride on our donkey', to lead our company, so that he could accomplish his purposes with the business. The CEOs realized that they were no longer the owners of their businesses and took on the role of a manager of Jesus' business! The Bible calls this 'stewardship.' A steward is the manager of the assets of someone else - in this case, the assets of the business were signed over to Jesus' ownership. What a liberating way to do business! Every decision was be made together with the new owner, the Lord himself. And he knows so much more about doing business and can do so much more than we can ever pray for or imagine!

The King is coming again, and he demands lordship over his enterprise. And that is exactly what "donkey business" is all about.

Becoming different

Will owned a large manufacturing company. Early one morning, Will was greeted at his office door by his plant manager, whose name was John. Without comment, John submitted his resignation, effective immediately. Will was devastated; for the past five years he had been grooming John to become president of his company.

When he questioned John about his reasons for leaving, John refused to discuss them. Will just couldn't understand it. He paid John more than anyone else in the company, including himself. But nothing would change John's mind. Will asked John to stay at least long enough to hire and train a new plant manager, but John angrily refused. Since John had been such a good friend, Will held a company going-away party and gave John a substantial severance bonus.

Three months later, John's reasons for leaving became apparent: He had opened his own company and copied Will's best-selling product. In time, John's company grew, becoming Will's leading competitor.

Later, Will learned that there was a design problem with one of John's new products and that several lawsuits were being filed against John's company. Now Will had forgiven John and had continued to pray for him on a regular basis.

He felt strongly that the Lord wanted him to reach out to John, so he bought one of John's products, tested it, and discovered the problem. Then amazingly, he told his engineers to find a way to fix it. After making and testing the necessary modifications, Will called John and told him how to solve his problem.

Radical Christianity? That's what some would say. Stupidity? That's what others would say. Only time will tell how John will respond to this act of unconditional Christ-like love. The results are not Will's responsibility. His responsibility, like ours, is to do what the Lord wants him to do.

When the Lord starts taking control of your business life things change. I think the first to change is your attitude to people. You no longer see them as employees to work for you, or competitors who make life difficult for you. You see them as Jesus sees them; as people to serve, so that they can reach their full God-given potential.

At our business, our critical success factor was not profit, sales or return on investment, but the number of people we could hire. We wanted people to come under our sphere of influence, so that they could first of all, get to know something about Jesus. We prayed for each employee in our weekly prayer time that they would come closer to Jesus. Then, our next goals were that they should be able to develop professionally. We spent more than our competitors on training. Then, we wanted them to grow relationally and also financially.

When Jesus rides on your donkey, your priorities change to reflect Jesus' priorities. These are clearly stated in his mission statement in Mark 10:45. "For even the Son of Man did not come to be served, but to serve, and to give his life as a ransom for many."

THE TIED-UP DONKEY

3

Our metaphor of donkey business continues at Jesus' triumphal entry into Jerusalem. "Go into the village over there," he said to his disciples. "As soon as you enter it, you will see a donkey tied there, with its colt beside it. Untie them and bring them to me. If anyone asks what you are doing, just say, 'The Lord needs them,' and he will immediately let you take them" (Matt. 21:2–3 nlt).

The donkey was tied up to a post. It could not run off until the owner came with a job for it to do. It had to carry a load or take someone to a destination. So, the donkey had to be freed, untied, to achieve its goal, to be used for the purpose for which it was created, to perform the duty of a 'beast of burden.' Moreover, in Mark's gospel we read that the donkey was tied up at a crossroad. The owner had a choice—to let the donkey go, or to keep it for himself. What would you have done?

I can see this donkey as a symbol of a present-day enterprise, not in tune with God's plan, tied down to the world's system and therefore not in a position to serve toward the goals God intended for it. Do you feel tied down, not really having the sense that you are going anywhere, not being able to do that for which the business was created? Perhaps your business is tied down with such heavy debt or other problems that it has stagnated. As long as your company remains tethered, it will be unfit for God's use, and you will struggle to discern God's will for it. So, set it free to be used by the Master for his purposes!

Enslaved

Issachar received a prophecy from his father, Jacob: "Issachar is a sturdy donkey, resting between two saddle packs. When he sees how good the countryside is and how pleasant the land, he will bend his shoulder to the load and submit himself to hard labor" (Gen. 49:14–15 nlt). This passage indicates that Issachar and his tribe allowed themselves to become a slave. He was strong and seemingly successful. Still, he rested on his laurels, trusted in his abilities, grew comfortable with his possessions—and ended up enslaved.

I have heard many a businessman, frustrated by the burden of debt, call out, "I feel like a slave to the bank! They lend me an umbrella when the sky is clear, but when the rain comes they immediately want it back!" A common cause of slavery in business is an unhealthy leveraging, the balance between your assets and your borrowings. The pressure to perform in order to pay back a potentially crippling debt can prevent the business from being available to do what God is asking.

I am glad that I learned this early during my career. I had the privilege to hear the late and great Dr. Frits Philips of the Dutch electronics conglomerate speak at one of our meetings for Christians in business. He always maintained that the ratio of assets to borrowings must remain healthy, never exceeding 50:50, so that if you cannot meet your obligations for any reason, you could liquidate some assets and pay off your debts. In his time at Philips, they had a ratio of debt to assets of no more than 20% or so. An excessive debt burden is one of the main reasons businesses are tied down these days and not useful for God's kingdom. Too much outside capital, however seemingly useful, can make it impossible for a business owner to be free to be able to make certain decisions in answer to God's call.

Idol Promises

Moreover, the donkey can be loaded down with all different kinds of burdens. "Bel bows down, Nebo stoops low; their idols are borne by beasts of burden. The images that are carried about are burdensome, a burden for the weary. They stoop and bow down together; unable to rescue the burden, they themselves go off into captivity." (Isa. 46:1–2)

Bel and Nebo were Babylonian gods. Isaiah pictured these idols becoming an unbearable weight on the backs of their donkeys, so that in the end the whole load collapsed and had to be towed away. Bel is the Babylonian word for "lord" and Nebo was his son. Nebo means, "to learn." Their names can be seen in the form of the Babylonian names Belshazzar and Nebuchadnezzar. The meanings of the names of the idols on the donkey's backs lead us to ask two very penetrating questions: "Who is Lord?" and "From whom are we learning?"

Are we freed from the idols that have taken over the Lord's place in our company? The idols that we carry around so ceremoniously, ultimately form such a heavy burden in our companies. We learn a lot more about these idols when God asks a few verses later; "To whom will you compare me or count me equal? To whom will you liken me that we may be compared? Some pour out gold from their bags and weigh out silver on the scales; they hire a goldsmith to make it into a god, and they bow down and worship it. They lift it to their shoulders and carry it; they set it up in its place, and there it stands. From that spot it cannot move. Though one cries out to it, it does not answer; it cannot save him from his troubles." (Isa. 46:5–7). If money is the primary purpose of our business, then focusing on money can open the door for the money god, mammon, to come in and motivate us to serve it, and not God! "No one can serve two masters. For you will hate one and love the other; you will be devoted to one and despise the other. You cannot serve God and be enslaved to money." (Matthew 6:24 nlt).

One of the characteristics of an idol is that it does not deliver what it promises. What it promises looks good but is in fact an empty shell. In Psalm 115:4–8, we read about the illusion of an idol: "Their idols are silver and gold, made by the hands of men. They have mouths, but cannot speak, eyes, but they cannot see; they have ears, but cannot hear, noses, but they cannot smell; they have hands, but cannot feel, feet, but they cannot walk; nor can they utter a sound with their throats. Those who make them will be like them and so will all who trust in them."

Business idols promise financial well-being, but only deliver at great cost. Over and over again we attempt to remake the golden calf, and we expect to get answers to all our problems from the god of money. But God invites us to learn from him: "Listen to me, descendants of Jacob, all you who remain in Israel. I have cared for you since you were born. Yes, I carried you before you were born. I will be your God throughout your lifetime—until your hair is white with age. I made you, and I will care for you. I will carry you along and save you." (Isa. 46:3–4 nlt)

Yes, God wants to teach us his ways, but before we can experience God's activities throughout our company, we must perceive what we need to be released from. We can start this process by asking two questions: "Who's in charge of your business?" and "What place does money hold in your business?" Let's look at each question in depth.

Who's in charge here?

The answer to our first question is typically "I am." Entrepreneurs are known to have incredibly big egos. Some say it's a requirement for an entrepreneur to be successful in business. In the English language ego is an acronym for "Edging God Out." It means relegating God to the periphery, making him irrelevant to daily affairs.

In recent times we have witnessed some admirable success stories and also some spectacular failures. I remember the bankruptcy of a very large Flemish software company, once at the very top of their market for speech and language software. One moment the CEO was manager of the year; shortly after their demise he was treated like dirt.

Fast Company is a hard-hitting, fast-paced magazine for businesspeople in the twenty-first century. I read an intriguing article called, "7 Habits of Spectacularly Un-successful Executives" by Sydney Finkelstein. In it he wrote, "The past few years have witnessed some admirable business successes and some exceptional failures—think Arthur Anderson, Rubbermaid, and Schwinn Bicycle, as well as a collection of former highfliers—think Enron, Tyco, and WorldCom. Behind each of these failures stands a towering figure: a CEO or business leader who will long be remembered for being spectacularly unsuccessful."

Hardly anyone gets a chance to destroy so much value without demonstrating the potential for creating it as the CEO. Most of the great destroyers of value are people of unusual intelligence and talent. They show personal magnetism and often inspire others. They are the men and women whose faces appear on the covers of esteemed business periodicals like Fortune and Forbes. "What is the secret of their incredibly destructive powers?" Finkelstein asked. Ironically, each of the "seven habits" identified by Finkelstein represents a quality that is widely admired in the business world. In fact, business does not merely tolerate these qualities; it celebrates and encourages them. These habits of entrepreneurs are as follows:

1. They see themselves and their companies as dominating their environment.

2. They identify so completely with their company that there is no clear boundary between their personal interests and their corporation's interests.

3. They think they have all the answers.

4. They ruthlessly eliminate anyone who isn't 100 percent behind them.

5. They are consummate spokespersons obsessed with the company image.

6. They underestimate obstacles.

7. They stubbornly rely on what worked for them in the past.

Finkelstein commented that leaders with these habits, "tend to see people as instruments to be used, as materials to be molded, or as audiences for their performances.... Being a CEO of a sizable corporation today is probably the closest thing to being king of your own country—and that's a dangerous, and sometimes self-destructive, title to assume."

Reading these indictments of abusive leaders, it is easy to be judgmental and condemning. But the Bible tells us, "No temptation has seized you except what is common to man" (1 Cor. 10:13). In other words, given the right time, place, and circumstances, any one of us could be tempted to do anything. So, regardless of whether you are the CEO of a company, a rising leader, a manager, or even someone just getting started in the business and professional world, study these habits. Learn to recognize them. And be honest; if you find yourself guilty of one or more of these habits, admit it and do what you must to change it.

I saved a clipping from a report in the London Times, describing the rise and fall of a young CEO, "one of British industry's rising stars.… the resignation will come as a massive blow to him, and it will take him a considerable time to think things over. He is a person who sheltered behind his pride and his ego. He had to be successful—but just as important; he had to be seen to be successful." Pride comes before a fall—and this man fell a long way!

What Place Does Money hold in Your Business?

The second question God has for us from Isaiah 46 is "What place does money hold in your business?" Is it just a means of exchange, or is it an idol? Does it serve a purpose, or does it exercise power? Jesus unmasked the power behind money and gave it a name, saying explicitly, "No servant can serve two masters. Either he will hate the one and love the other, or he will be devoted to the one and despise the other. You cannot serve both God and mammon" (Luke 16:13). Jesus is unmasking the spiritual power behind money, calling it by a name, and describing this as a major competitor to God for our devotion and allegiance.

Jacques Ellul, a professor emeritus of sociology at the University of Bordeaux in France wrote in his classic work. 'Money and Power,' that the idea grew among us that money equals blessing. That is not always the case! So we grant money a spiritual value. He went on to say that Jesus wants to open our eyes to the fact that money represents a dynamic power. Money exercises power and has the ability to move us in a certain direction.

My experience in doing business, in common with many other entrepreneurs, is that God can bless us just as much by keeping money from us as by giving us financial success! The enemy of our souls, however, wants to convince us that money is indispensable and a precondition for blessing. When God withholds money from us, that is our inviation to experience God's correction and leadership!

In the verses preceding Luke 16:13, Jesus contrasts the qualities of the person who serves money with the qualities of the individual who serves God.

First of all, the one who serves God will be honest in all things—large and small. The one who serves money, whose highest goal is to amass more will likely be dishonest: "Whoever can be trusted with very little can also be trusted with much, and whoever is dishonest with very little will also be dishonest with much" (Luke 16:10). Money is only a little thing, only a means in God's hand that he wants us to use to test our trustworthiness.

Second, the servant of God will be trustworthy in all things—major and minor. "If you have not been trustworthy in handling worldly wealth, who will trust you with true riches?" (Luke 16:11). Jesus didn't even consider money to be "true riches." The one who serves money does not acknowledge its source or the fact that it is no measure of real wealth.

Third, the person who serves God realizes he is simply a steward, a manager of the money, skills, talents, and other gifts God has given. And God expects him to be faithful with what has been entrusted to him. Jesus said, "If you have not been trustworthy with someone else's property, who will give you property of your own?" (Luke 16:12).

Mother Teresa was very explicit in her statement: "by being in touch with money, one loses touch with God." It is up to us as Christian businesspeople to learn how to use money the right way, which is to honor God!

The ties that bind

When Jesus wanted to use the donkey for his own purposes, he told the disciples that the donkey was tied up. Our businesses, too, may be tied up and unavailable for God's work. Here are some ropes can so easily bind us.

Serving the wrong master. A ship with two captains will go nowhere. In the same way two leaders in a company lead to confusion and frustration. You need to choose: 'Do I want to serve God or money?' It is essential for a Christian entrepreneur to keep the focus of the business on God rather than on money, and to learn how to respond to the calling of God. Joshua, the man God chose to lead his people into the Promised Land, said, "If you refuse to serve the Lord, then choose today whom you will serve. Would you prefer the gods your ancestors served beyond the Euphrates? Or will it be the gods of the Amorites in whose land you now live? But as for me and my family [my business], we will serve the Lord" (Josh. 24:15 nlt).

Over-indebtedness. Too much borrowing is a rope by which we often are bound and even paralyzed. Do you feel, as I have in the past, that you are being swallowed by a "borrow constrictor"? Do you set off to the office each day singing like Cinderella's seven dwarves in the Disney film, "I owe, I owe, it's off to work I go"? Donkey business involves recognizing God as the source of our capital, provided we first seek his kingdom, because therein is an incredible promise: "Seek the Kingdom of God above all else, and live righteously, and he will give you everything you need" (Matt. 6:33 nlt). I am convinced that this also means he will provide working capital and sufficient cash flow for our daily needs. I have known many Christian entrepreneurs who refused to borrow from the bank to grow their businesses. It is amazing how the creativity given by God can shine through when we are not dependent on the bank for financing, but on God!

Workaholism. Addicted to work, making long hours, being under a delusion that the job demands it, can bind us and keep us from serving God. According to an article in the German magazine Psychology Today, "Workaholics, despite making long hours, feel inferior and dissatisfied. They miss the feeling of belonging, of recognition; and to fill the emptiness they believe they have to work long hours to create a feeling of security." Please remember that the love of Jesus and his acceptance do not depend on performance! Through the prophet Isaiah God said, "You are precious to me. You are honored, and I love you" (Isa. 43:4 nlt). God's love does not depend on our performance! A good friend is Dave Rae, who was a VP at Apple for many years. He always set a limit of 45 hours a week, despite the constant pressure to improve results. He said, "If I cannot get my job done in that time, I am either doing the wrong things, or not doing them right." Despite a very responsible job in a dynamic multinational, he always had time for his family, friends and Christian ministry.

Weariness. Allowing people to pile up the burden of many tasks on your shoulders and not saying no, drags us down and keeps us from God's service. Doing is no substitute for being. Choosing the right things to do, and not submitting to the 'tyranny of the urgent,' is an art. Jesus invites us to join him in his work when we are weary and burdened: "Come to me, all of you who are weary and carry heavy burdens, and I will give you rest. Take my yoke upon you. Let me teach you, because I am humble and gentle at heart, and you will find rest for your souls. For my yoke is easy to bear, and the burden I give you is light" (Matt. 11:28–30 nlt). By inviting us to take his "yoke," he is inviting us into a working partnership. I have my unique role and Jesus also has his unique role. My part is to be faithful in getting to know and carry out Jesus' instructions. Jesus role is to provide, lead, guide, encourage and instruct. I can't imagine a better business associate, can you? I can never do what ony Jesus can do; and he will also not do what I must do.

Worries. Will the business survive without you? Most businessmen are under the excessive impression that they are indispensable and cannot be missed from their business. I am sure you can take necessary time off, but you have to plan it very well. Building in a quiet time to be alone with the Lord gives us the opportunity to hear his voice. Paul wrote, "Do not be anxious about anything, but in everything, by prayer and petition, with thanksgiving, present your requests to God. And the peace of God, which transcends all understanding, will guard your hearts and your minds in Christ Jesus" (Phil. 4:6–7). In other words, do not worry!

Wage slavery. Are you unable to change jobs because of financial needs? I remember talking to an Italian high-level executive, living in a beautiful villa in an expensive part of town. Speaking to his wife one day, I said, "you must be very happy here. What a lovely home, you have." She replied, "Hmmm, not so happy. I am very homesick." I said, "So why not move back to Italy? "She replied, "We cannot move back because we have a large mortgage and an expensive lifestyle. We could never maintain this all if we should move back. I feel like I am living in a golden cage!"

Are you living and working in a "golden cage" from which you cannot really move because your financial commitments and maintaining your standard of living will not allow it? Plan to become debt-free, and scale down your lifestyle. Remember, God is the source of provision for your everyday needs, if you seek his kingdom first (see Matt. 6:33).

Wrong priorities. Is it possible to free yourself sufficiently to be available for God's work? Ted DeMoss, as president of CBMC (Christian Business Men's Committees) used to say, "the most important thing is to keep the most important thing the most important thing." When we put God first, our other priorities will begin to fall into place.

Exclusively Focused on success

This last "rope"—an exclusive focus on success—can be such a major problem for Christian entrepreneurs that I'd like to address it in a bit more detail. It was my privilege to have Dr. Siegfried Buchholz as my mentor. After a long career as a director of the chemical company BASF, he is now a leading management consultant and coach in Vienna, Austria. He conducted a survey of entrepreneurs who made their business success the highest priority in their lives. He discovered a red line running through their behavior that resulted in their falling into a self-made trap.

The symptoms included the following:

1. They exclude their spouses and their children from their professional life, switching off a very important source of support and energy.

2. They shrink their social environment and substitute good friends with customers and colleagues, destroying their most important personal safety net.

3. They believe they can increase their productivity by increasing their working time and pressure, and they lose their own personal identity.

4. They discard those around them who give open and sincere feedback, eliminating important corrections and crucial information.

5. They concentrate on those areas of work that have given them success so far, narrowing their horizon, which makes them increasingly unwilling and unable to change.

6. They discard the highest authority (God) from their life and become complacent, thus losing contact with reality and becoming dangerously helpless in crisis situations.

"Things which matter most must never be at the mercy of things which matter least." These words from German author Goethe sketch a dilemma we all face. This dilemma was described by Charles Hummel in his defining work, 'The Tyranny of the Urgent,' which described how the urgent tasks of everyday work crowd out the most important activities of our lives.

Don't Let Yourself Become chained

Do you ever feel burdened down? An old story tells that God created the donkey and instructed him: "You will be a donkey; you will work hard from dusk till dawn and carry heavy loads. You will eat grass and be called stubborn. You will live fifty years." The donkey replied, "It is too much to live like that for fifty years. Please give me twenty years." And that is what happened.

God created the dog and told him, "You will guard man and be his most loyal friend. You will eat the leftovers from his table, and live twenty-five years." But the dog said, "Please, Lord, to live like that for twenty-five years is too much. Please make it no more than ten years." And so it happened.

The Lord created the monkey and said to him, "You are a monkey. You will swing from tree to tree and play foolish tricks. You will be funny, make people laugh, and live twenty years." And the monkey replied, "Lord, twenty years is too long to be the clown of the world. Please make it no more than ten years." And so it happened.

Finally, God created man and said to him, "You are a man, the only rational being on earth. You will use your intelligence to rule over all the creatures in the world and you will live for twenty years." The man replied, "Lord, to live only twenty years as a human being is too short. Please give me the twenty years that the donkey rejected, the fifteen years the dog refused, and the ten years the monkey did not want." And so it happened.

The man got twenty years to live like a man; then thirty years to get married, have children, and carry heavy loads—to live like a donkey; fifteen years to guard his home and eat leftovers—to live like a dog; and finally ten years to be the clown amusing his grandchildren—to live like a monkey. And so it happened!

Jesus calls us to untie the donkey and let it loose. Then we are free to enjoy life and to be used by the Lord and to love and serve him with all our hearts, souls, minds, and strength.

Donkeys need to be untied. Our careers, businesses, assets, finances, and possessions must be released from being tied up and being ineffective for God. It is a real art to become freely available for God's donkey business! Follow Jesus and become truly free! "Jesus said to the people who believed in him, 'You are truly my disciples if you remain faithful to my teachings. And you will know the truth, and the truth will set you free'" (John 8:31–32).

Once the donkey is free from the ropes that bind and burden it down, it must be connected to the one place where it can grow and become all it was created to be. The next chapter provides the details.

THE DONKEY AND THE VINE

4

In the last chapter I told you that your donkey needs to be untied, but I didn't give you the entire story. Yes, your donkey needs to be freed from serving the wrong master, from the burden of excessive debt, from worries, and the other ropes mentioned. However, donkeys weren't created to live on their own and be self-sufficient. They need to be attached, connected, to that which will strengthen and direct them. Only then can they fulfil their purpose in life!

The patriarch Jacob gave the following interesting description to his son Judah, who was an ancestor of David and out of which family Jesus came; "He will tether his donkey to a vine, his colt to the choicest branch" (Gen. 49:11). What a wonderful invitation!

In an agricultural economy, a vine is a precious and valuable asset. It contributes to the wealth of the farmer and offers shade and nourishment. Now, a donkey is a herbivore, a plant eater. Can it be good advice to tie a donkey to a vine? Will the donkey not eat the vine's leaves, or pull stubbornly away from the vine, tearing its branches? In like manner, a business can also so easily eat up or destroy its own assets. So, literally tying a donkey to a vine appears to be a bad idea. Symbolically, however, tying a donkey (business) to the Vine (Jesus) can represent a business that's well and truly nourished—one that bears fruit.

The Vine

The vine is a biblical metaphor for the source of fruit in the Christian life: the Lord Jesus himself, whose Father looks after it and prunes it, so that it bears a lot of fruit! How can I access, in my business, the wisdom that comes from above? How can I control myself and lead others? How can my company be used for God's purposes? How can I get the same passion for people that Jesus had?

The answer is to tie your donkey to the Vine! Park your donkey—your business, your assets, your people, at the true Vine so that your business, connected to the Vine, can produce an abundance of fruit! The dynamic energy and the life of the Vine will flow through the donkey, through your enterprise, to bear fruit to the glory of God.

Jesus spoke explicitly about the fact that we cannot bear spiritual fruit unless we stay connected to the vine. "I am the vine; you are the branches. If a man remains in me and I in him, he will bear much fruit; apart from me you can do nothing" (John 15:5).

To tie your donkey to the vine means that you are willing to let God prune you and all the activities of your company in order to bear fruit. Jesus said, "I am the true vine, and my Father is the gardener. He cuts off every branch in me that bears no fruit, while every branch that does bear fruit he prunes so that it will be even more fruitful" (John 15:1–2).

Spiritual blessing from God often begins with pruning. I see many entrepreneurs come to believe in the Lord. They express enthusiasm and gratitude for their new life with the Lord and expect God to bless them right from the start! They forget that the pruning comes before the process of growth. I have often heard young Christian businessmen say, "I thought everything would be going my way now that I've become a Christian, but now I encounter more problems than before."

This observation is correct, and it is just what God wants. The owner of the vineyard has to work hard, tidying up, removing rocks, breaking the hard soil, weeding, and clipping the branches before any fruit appears. Sometimes a whole company has to be cleared away if the roots are rotten.

My mind goes back to a businessman who used to do interior decorating for brothels and other property connected to the underworld in Amsterdam. After his conversion he refused to continue this work, even being threatened to do so at gunpoint! His business quickly went under, but he himself started growing in his faith and trusting God for a new business. He started another company, again in interior decorating, but this time built on a better foundation and with a different customer base. He never went back to his old market.

Judah—a Picture of a Businessman

The arch father Jacob, prophesied about his son Judah, "He will tie his donkey to the vine." Born the fourth son of Leah and Jacob, Judah's name means 'Glory to the Lord.' This name reflects the first goal of a Christian entrepreneur: to bring glory to God, to uphold God's name and reputation so that people will honor and accept the Lord and all his ways. As business people, we know that your name and reputation needs protecting! It takes years to build up but can be destroyed in seconds. Lifting up God's name in the marketplace and maintaining his reputation is of primary importance!

That was not easy for Judah with a father like Jacob. Jacob, the deceiver, exercised such a strong influence over his sons that they too became deceivers. Maybe that is one of the biggest problems people often have with Christians in business: What they say is not always commensurate with what they do. When talking with non-Christians, this is often the objection I encounter: "They say one thing but do another; that's hypocrisy." To demonstrate integrity, however, means to say what you do and do what you say. Your business dealings must be in harmony with your walk with the Lord.

I will never forget taking a guest to an outreach dinner where he met a business associate with whom he was in conflict. This colleague was the leader of the local group of Christian businessmen. My guest exclaimed, "If that's a Christian, then count me out!" He was referring to his colleague's manner of doing business, which was completely opposite of what he expected from a Christian.

This following report was published in USA Today. The names have been changed.

"Bill Eagleton stated he was worth more than $1 billion. Now the company he has founded is in shambles, his debts far exceed his once unfathomable assets and he's all but bankrupt. But whether he's teaching Sunday school, drinking beer at his favorite nightspots or calling former colleagues, those who've talked with the former Worldweb CEO in the past few weeks say that one thing resonates: he acts like nothing has happened.… Eagleton is clearly buoyed by his religious faith (he's a born-again Christian…). When he's out socially … he talks about how ill a bartender is, what's new in another's business, his church and tennis.… On Sundays Eagleton is at Westwood Baptist Church, where he teaches Sunday school for an hour … and every week or two, he and his wife visit Tyson's, usually for lobster and drinks.… John Caldwell, a minister at Eagleton's church, says members want to give him the benefit of the doubt.

Eagleton appears to be a devout Baptist. "I am a child of the King, and the King is still King Jesus, and I am absolutely content and happy." Still, he flouts some of the basic tenets of the religion, which, Caldwell says, opposes divorce, infidelity and drinking. At Worldweb, Eagleton was known to stay up drinking with colleagues until the early hours of the morning, even before board meetings, which he always opened with a prayer.… Eagleton and his wife of about 30 years, Jane, divorced about five years ago. He openly courted Cathy, a former top Worldweb sales associate, while the two were married to others … yet he teaches a Sunday school class for young couples interested in learning about the gospel and how it relates to marriage. "It is so inappropriate the way he wears his Christian banner," says Johnson real-estate agent George Long, "The people down here refuse to accept the hypocrisy." If any of his apparent incongruities are bothering him, Eagleton isn't showing it."

This is by no means an isolated case. Do you ever wonder why the world isn't taking Christianity seriously?

Judah's business dealings, too, showed a discrepancy between his stated beliefs and his actions. In Genesis we read that when the brothers, Jacob's sons, wanted to kill their brother Joseph, Judah came up with a business-like solution: "What will we gain if we kill our brother and cover up his blood? Come, let's sell him to the Ishmaelites and not lay our hands on him; after all, he is our brother, our own flesh and blood. His brothers agreed" (Gen. 37:26–27). When the Ishmaelite merchants from Gilead passed by with their caravan, the brothers pulled Joseph up out of the pit and sold him for twenty pieces of silver. The Ishmaelites then took Joseph into Egypt and sold him as a slave to an Egyptian official. Not such a good trader after all, because the current price for a slave in the region was thirty silver coins! A few thousand years later, Judas did better. He got thirty silver coins when selling our Lord Jesus. In both situations, love for business and money took precedence over love for the Lord God.

Judah also had problems during his marriage. He left his father's home to marry a girl from Canaan, a girl not from his own faith, which God had forbidden. He lost his eldest son, because the boy was so sinful. Judah also had problems with his second son, who did not want to obey him, and so he lost him too. Once, he thought he was sharing his bed with a prostitute, but it turned out to be his daughter-in-law. His family was all misery.

A change occurred in Judah's life when he started to trade well in Egypt. His father sent him there to buy food for the family. He and his brothers were accused of theft, and his youngest brother, Benjamin, was taken hostage. Judah managed to bring Benjamin back to his father, and ultimately take the whole family into safety. During his stay in Egypt, Judah was converted; he confessed his guilt to Joseph and received forgiveness from Joseph for all the wrongdoings he and his brothers had committed against Joseph. Joseph, who is seen in the Bible as a type of Jesus (for example, both were beloved sons, both were rejected, tempted, and finally exalted), sent Judah on his way with a new commission from Pharaoh. "Pharaoh said to Joseph,

'Tell your brothers, "Do this: Load your animals and return to the land of Canaan and bring your father and your families back to me. I will give you the best of the land of Egypt and you can enjoy the fat of the land" (Gen. 45:17–18). Also, Joseph gave his brothers gifts for their father, "And this is what he sent to his father: ten donkeys loaded with the best things of Egypt, and ten female donkeys loaded with grain and bread and other provisions for his journey" (Gen. 45:23).

Likewise, when God sends us on our way with a new commission, he also supplies us liberally with all we need to do the job he has given us!

Jesus—the Ultimate Business Partner

To "tie your donkey to the vine" means to form a partnership with Jesus himself. "Become my partner," Jesus invites us, "accept a commission from me and share my work. I will carry the load with you. Learn from me how meaningful your new work can be. You will experience my humble power working through you and find out how restful it is to work with me! My assignments are not difficult, and my work is not heavy!" (Matt.11:28–29, author's paraphrase).

Jesus didn't use many adjectives to describe his character. In Matthew 11, however, he says he is "gentle and humble in heart." Elsewhere the Bible says he entered Jerusalem "gentle and riding on a donkey" (Zech. 9:9; Matt. 21:5). These are expressions not often heard in modern business life. But when Jesus takes charge of your donkey, people will notice your meekness and humility. Meekness is not a characteristic typically associated with businessmen. We tend more to be proud, convinced of our ability and assured of our future success. Nevertheless, humility and meekness are pre-conditional to fully experiencing the life of Christ and they come as a result of tying your donkey to the true Vine.

The Danish sculptor Bertel Thorwaldsen was asked to make a statue of Christ blessing with outstretched hands. He first made a model out of pliable clay. He left his studio, which was near the beach, to let the clay dry overnight. During the night, a mist came in from the sea, and the moisture penetrated into the clay and substantially changed the appearance of the figure. When the sculptor came back the next day, he was shocked and exclaimed that his work had been destroyed. The hands, previously stretched out above the figure to bless, were now hanging down in an inviting gesture. The head of Christ, at first turned upward to heaven, now looked down onto the earth, so that most of the face was hidden.

Thorwaldsen kept staring at the model and suddenly realized that this was how the statue had to be. "Indeed," he said, "when you want to see the face of Christ, you have to humble yourself and bow down before him."

Behind the image of the self-assured, strong businessman another smaller part of the person hides. Sue Erikson Boland wrote, "I reached the conclusion that every overtly powerful, self-assured, haughty public image covers shame." Later in the same article she said, "Pride is a form of narcissism and a defense against shame—a realization that the inner person has serious defects. One is just not good enough."

Professor Dr. Manfred Kets de Vries of the French Business School INSEAD near Paris, France, described the inner longing for success and recognition, very common among entrepreneurs, as being a direct result of rejection at a younger age. This often forms the motivation of entrepreneurs to show their parents (whether alive or dead) that they can succeed and excel, thereby bringing them the love and esteem they never previously received.

A few years ago I had the privilege to mentor the elder son of a rich project developer. The son suffered a great deal under the unexpressed expectations of his very dominant father. This suffering only slowly disappeared when he stepped out of the family business and moved to another city. Only then did he start to develop as an individual, and not as an extension of his father, constantly striving to measure up to these felt expectations.

Binding ourselves to the Vine, to Jesus Christ, breaks this spirit of inadequacy and opens up a new source of energy and a spirit of acceptance. The humbleness and meekness of Jesus will then be offered to us. Jesus stated, "Blessed are the meek, for they will inherit the earth" (Matt. 5:5). It is a misconception to think that meekness means weakness. The opposite is true! Meekness is strength under control. Meekness comes to the surface when strong people choose to serve instead of exercising their power. It forces you not to take yourself too seriously or to seek too much recognition from people. The meek are seriously surprised when they find themselves in the center of attention. They seek the best in their fellow human beings and desire to create conditions for maximum development in others.

The Bible describes Moses as meek, but he was a powerful leader who successfully shepherded millions of people across a harsh desert and to the edge of the Promised Land. Meekness is power, for it draws energy, self-esteem, and acceptance from a new source: its connection with Jesus.

Park your donkey at the vine and let the vital power of the vine flow freely through your donkey to bring about humbleness and meekness.

Jim Collins talks in his bestseller "Good to Great" about the importance of the kind of meekness that Jesus showed. The first characteristic mentioned in his book is what Collins calls the "level 5 leader." Such a leader shows seemingly opposite qualities of modesty and willpower, meekness and firmness. These leaders adhere to what he calls their "window and mirror principle." They look out the window to see who to praise for the success of the project, and then look in the mirror when it comes to assigning responsibility. The meekness of Jesus also consists of willpower and firmness combined with a responsibility toward his Father and passion for others.

Jesus said, "Blessed are the meek." Blessed means that all of God's resources are available to us—his approval, his acceptance, his energy, and his power. So, come to the vine and enjoy everything God gives from his goodness.

The Vine—a change agent

"Want to break in your spirited young horse? Take a twelve-inch-long rope and tie it to a donkey. Within forty-eight hours it will be as quiet as a lamb." This advice came from an old Irish horse trainer who knew that the stubbornness of the donkey would not yield to the antics of a feisty horse much bigger than himself. The donkey went where it wanted to, and the horse just had to learn to submit and follow. And it did!

You and I, stubborn Christians in business, can also experience this in a positive way by tying our donkey to the Vine.

Jesus said, "Come to me, all of you who are weary and carry heavy burdens, and I will give you rest. Take my yoke upon you. Let me teach you, because I am humble and gentle at heart, and you will find rest for your souls. For my yoke is easy to bear, and the burden I give you is light" (Matt. 11:28–30 nlt). The Lord invites us to be tied to him by a twelve-inch piece of rope, or to work with him in a "yoke" carrying equally the burden of our work! We will then learn to follow Jesus and experience him working in close proximity.

Conversely, my friend Hans said to me one day, "I can't believe how irritable and angry I have become. I used to let my values and faith influence my decision making, but now it all seems to circle around monthly profits, share prices and cash flow." That morning he had realized he didn't like the man he saw in the mirror. He had become part of the corporate culture. Research shows how quickly we become absorbed into the corporate environment, through pressure to modify our attitudes, expectations, and behavior. Immersed in the culture of business, we can easily lose sight of our values and principles. And being yoked to a partner who doesn't share your values can seriously affect your spiritual health!

A person changed by Christ, however, changes his environment. We know that when we stay closely connected to Christ and share his yoke, we then start to experience his power flowing through our donkey, our business. This in turn has a formative effect on our surroundings, resulting in biblical values becoming daily practice and changing people for the best.

The apostle Paul took a line from a popular Greek tragedy and wrote it into Scripture for insertion in our mental database: "Bad company corrupts good character" (1 Cor. 15:33). The wise King Solomon said, "He who walks with the wise grows wise, but a companion of fools suffers harm" (Prov. 13:20). "Learn from me," Jesus invites. Being a lifelong learner in a learning organization, enjoying the power and wisdom of the Creator himself, is a real privilege!

Someone got very good Irish advice at a renowned horse-racing event when he asked, "Whatever is that old nag doing in this race?" The answer was, "I know he has no chance of winning, but the association will do him good." Being tied to the Vine assures our business of association with the best possible business partner - the Lord Jesus Christ.

THE REDEEMED DONKEY

5

Who is Peter Chamor?" This is a question laughingly asked by a rabbi of his pupils to explain a fascinating commandment from the Torah. Peter Chamor is not a person but two Hebrew words referring to a Jewish custom meaning "the initiation of the donkey."

We read in Exodus 13:13 the commandment to "Redeem with a lamb every firstborn donkey, but if you do not redeem it, break its neck. Redeem every firstborn among your sons."

It seems that the donkey had a special status in the traditions of Israel. It is the only non-kosher animal from which the firstborn, belonging to the Lord, had to be redeemed. The first-born son of every Jew had to be redeemed for the service to the Lord by making substitutionary sacrifice. Male firstborn kosher animals were destined for the Lord and were sacrificed in the temple. However, the donkey was considered to be non-kosher and therefore could not be used as an acceptable offering. The owner had to redeem the donkey with a lamb, which was perfectly acceptable; the lamb was to be given to the priest instead of the donkey. In other words, if the donkey was not made acceptable to God by sacrificing a lamb in its place, it would be totally useless to God! In the same way everything we own, also a company, assets, career, ambition is made acceptable before God by the sacrifice of the Lamb of God, Jesus Christ.

Recently I read an explanation of Exodus 13:13 from a Jewish perspective. The writer suggested that the reason the donkey had to be sacrificed if not redeemed, could be found in a simple cost-profit analysis. A donkey is worth more money than a lamb. The Torah gives this command in such a way that not performing the mitzvah (the commandment) results in an economic punishment. By giving a lamb, you obey the commandment, perform a mitzvah, and you keep the donkey. By withholding a lamb, you commit an averah (a moral transgression) and you lose the donkey. The choice is yours. According to the Torah one could also give the equivalent in money. So, just a case of doing good business!

Incidentally, a reason for the redeeming of a donkey could very well come from Ezekiel 23:20 (nasb). The materialism of Egypt used by Israel in an adulterous way is compared here to "the flesh of donkeys." The Hebrew word for donkey— 'chamor'—is compared by rabbinical commentators to the word 'chomor'. This word means something like to be unbridled, to give oneself over to uncontrolled and undisciplined materialism.

So a kosher animal, a lamb, redeems the non-kosher donkey. This is an analogy of Israel being herded by a heavenly shepherd. The sanctification of the people occurs after their freedom from Egypt. They exchanged their materialistic donkeys for a spiritual life, acknowledging that the Lord is their shepherd and that the blood of the lamb has saved them. Jesus, the Lamb of God, bought and paid for us with his blood. Paul wrote, "You are not your own; you were bought at a price. Therefore, honor God with your body" (1 Cor. 6:19–20).

Jesus did this on the cross when he called out, "*Tetelestai!*" meaning "It is finished!" This word was used in Greek business in New Testament times, and when a bill was paid, the word 'tetelestai' was written on the invoice, which means 'paid in full.' This also applies to your business, which was bought and paid for by the precious blood of Jesus! So, donkey business has everything to do with the redemption of your business. God wants to use our donkey, business, assets, and company for his redeeming work.

I met a businessman after he'd had a successful year. In gratitude to God he decided to let his customers appreciate the meaning of being freed from debt. In December, as usual every month, he sent out his invoices. But this time he wrote on the bills "Paid in full!" And this year it meant about 10 percent of the annual turnover! In this way he wanted to demonstrate to his customers what Jesus did for us. Jesus paid our debt with God in full, and he delivered us so that we can become all he wants us to be. This businessman wanted to show his gratitude by his actions because he himself had received so much from God.

When the donkey was chosen, the priest spoke a special blessing. To realize that your business has been redeemed, that God has bought it with a Lamb, is quite a momentous occasion. I was invited to a dedication service in the office of a friend's business. This was led by his pastor, celebrating the fact that a change of ownership had taken place and dedicating the company to the new Owner!

I came across a study about the *'chamor,'* written by Rabbi Hillel Ben David. In it, he compared Abraham with Moses. Abraham used his donkey to take Isaac and his redeeming tools (wood, knife) to the mountain. Moses put his wife and children on a donkey and went on his way back to Egypt with the staff of God in his hand. Both men were leaders in the business of redemption. Next, the rabbi drew a comparison with the Messiah, for whom Jerusalem calls out with ecstatic joy, "Rejoice greatly, O Daughter of Zion! Shout, Daughter of Jerusalem! See, your king comes to you, righteous and having salvation, gentle and riding on a donkey, on a colt, the foal of a donkey" (Zech. 9:9). This is the ultimate redemption business. This enterprise will have succeeded completely when ultimately the Son of Man will come back to us not on a donkey, but on the clouds of heaven and in all his glory!

Carlos Vilhalba

Carlos Vilhalba collected many national awards as a renowned Sportsman in Guatemala. He had a small secret. No-one knew he was in deep financial trouble. His debt amounted to 900.000 dollars which was eating up his business like a cancer.

He signed up for a financial seminar and at the end of the day went home shocked. He had never heard the word of God applied to his life and his business in such a relevant way. He realized that he was not being a good manager of the blessings God entrusted to him. He decided that he was going to change the way he managed his business.

In a restaurant, his friend tried to probe for the spiritual roots of the problem. He asked Carlos about his assets and liabilities. He owned a very large empty building in Guatemala City; and it was fully paid for but completely empty. Carlos said that this was a very special building; for him it was the fulfilment of a dream. Carlos explained that when he was a little boy his family was extremely poor. Carlos was a little Shoe Shiner with Big Dreams! When cleaning the shoes of a rich businessman, he would say to himself, 'Carlos, one day you too will have your own Factory!'

That huge empty building was the fulfilment of his dream, that one day he will have his own Factory.

There was only one problem. The building had been sitting empty for several years now and all of his attempts to start production in his Factory had failed.

The next day at the seminar was going to be a life changing experience for Carlos. The topic of the night was ownership and stewardship.

The trainer explained that God owns it all through passages like Psalm 24:1 or first Chronicles 29:11,12. Even though this may sound familiar, saying that God owns it all is much easier than living it and surrendering to God, allowing him to be in control and trusting in His provision. This is one of the hardest things to do in life; switching from acting like an owner to acting like a manager. This is one of the true signs of maturity in a Christian. Emotional detachment to finances is a critical step to make in our journey to financial healing.

Carlos went home that night, walked straight to his bedroom and fell on his knees before the Lord. He suddenly realized that he had surrendered everything to the Lord except one thing, his dream. He had dedicated his life, his home his wife his family even a lot of things but Carlos was still holding on to the dream of being a Factory owner. The emotional attachment to his dream was not allowing him to behave like an administrator of God's possessions.

Carlos fell to the ground and surrendered to God what he considered the most precious possession he had in life - his childhood dream.

The following week, Carlos called a meeting with all of his creditors explained to them that he owned a very large building in Guatemala City. The building was completely empty and that he was ready to sell building, which was valued at 1.1 million dollars. He told its creditors he was willing to give it to them in exchange for all his debts. They didn't know what to say but after some deliberation they accepted the exchange and Carlos was set free from the bondage of debt.

Some months later, his country went through a major economic crisis which allowed Carlos not only to make money due to his good cash position, but also to purchase the business of some competitors. Carlos' financial success did not lie in his ability to make smart financial decisions. He would say without reservation that the secret was the life changing experience in realizing that he must behave each day as a trustee of God's possessions, acting as an administrator and manager and that God must be the absolute owner everything. Even to the point of owning his most cherished dreams!

Who is the owner?

We read in Luke 19:33, "As they were untying the colt, its owners asked them, "Why are you untying the colt?" Luke indicates that the young donkey probably had more than one owner, which was unusual in the Jewish community of that time.

Was the animal a special one, so precious it had to be bought by a syndicate, just as today a valuable racehorse is bought by a partnership as an investment? The Greek word used by Luke is "*kurios*," which means lord, or master, or to whom a thing belongs. We have our 'donkey,' our business, at our disposal— can we transfer ownership to the rightful Master because "he has need of it"?

The Bible teaches us that the marketplace is immensely influenced by individuals' desire for material wealth at any cost. Jesus warned us, "no one can serve two masters. Either he will hate the one and love the other, or he will be devoted to the one and despise the other. You cannot serve both God and Money" (Luke 16:13). A choice has to be made. Who are you serving as a company? It is either one or the other.

"Once you were dead because of your disobedience and your many sins. You used to live in sin, just like the rest of the world, obeying the devil—the commander of the powers in the unseen world. He is the spirit at work in the hearts of those who refuse to obey God. All of us used to live that way, following the passionate desires and inclinations of our sinful nature. By our very nature we were subject to God's anger, just like everyone else." (Eph. 2:1–3 nlt)

"But now, God saved you by his grace when you believed. And you can't take credit for this; it is a gift from God. Salvation is not a reward for the good things we have done, so none of us can boast about it. For we are God's masterpiece. He has created us anew in Christ Jesus, so we can do the good things he planned for us long ago." (Eph. 2:8–10 nlt)

There has to be a change of ownership. We receive new goals, new instructions from God. This applies to companies too; we get a new mission, a new goal, new core values, all prepared by God himself. Unfortunately, few entrepreneurs perceive this. They carry on under the influence of their desire for material wealth without realizing that God has already bought their company. They really do not want to know about such a takeover and want to stay owner of the company themselves.

I have always been fascinated by the fact that Jesus was sold for money—for thirty silver coins, in fact, the going price for a slave in those days. Why had Jesus to be sold? I think Jesus allowed himself just for once to come under the influence of human greed, so that by his death and resurrection the power of money could be broken once and for all. Paul wrote, "He canceled the record of the charges against us and took it away by nailing it to the cross. In this way, he disarmed the spiritual rulers and authorities. He shamed them publicly by his victory over them on the cross" (Col. 2:14–15).

The characteristic of the world's economy is "buying and selling." God's economy works in a different way, by "giving and receiving." Jesus broke the power of the world's economy by submitting himself to be sold for money, in order that he could teach us the true meaning of giving, introducing people to the principle of grace at work in the kingdom of God.

To tie your donkey to the vine means a change of ownership. Now your company, under the direction of the Holy Spirit, no longer has to be controlled by the inordinate desire for material wealth. Have you transferred your company to God?

I know many entrepreneurs who made a symbolic gesture by signing a kind of deed of sale, stating that all the shares have been transferred to the Lord our God. "This is the most liberating thing I've never done," Richard a good friend of mine told me. "My business now belongs to God! Instead of asking myself what to do next, now I first start to pray and ask Lord what are we going to do now? After all, Lord, it is now your money, your business, your co-worker, your problem?"

God's ownership

As Christians we should acknowledge God's ownership and effectively transfer ownership of our business or professional life to the Lord, as true disciples. "So therefore, any one of you who does not renounce all that he has cannot be my disciple." (Luke 14:33). Is that easy? Maybe, maybe not, but we must give up any claim to ownership. Sometimes the Lord will test our willingness to give up one of the very possessions that is most important to us.

The most vivid example of this in the Bible is when the Lord instructed Abraham, "Take your son, your only son Isaac, whom you love, and go to the land of Moriah, and offer him there as a burnt offering on one of the mountains of which I shall tell you." (Genesis 22:2). When Abraham obeyed, demonstrating his willingness to give up his most valuable possession, God responded with "Do not lay your hand on the boy or do anything to him, for now I know that you fear God, seeing you have not withheld your son, your only son, from me." (Genesis 22:12).

When we acknowledge God's ownership, every professional decision becomes a spiritual decision. We do have a large degree of freedom to make decisions, based on our experience, wisdom, counsel and the guidance of the Holy Spirit. No longer do we ask, "Lord, what do You want me to do with my business?" The question is restated, "Lord, what do You want me to do with Your business?" How is that for a pressure reliever? God is not distant, but wants to be intimately involved in your personal life and your professional life. He is an approachable shareholder, who loves to give his opinion, advice and direction, if you ask Him.

It is to the glory of God that He owns the business and that we serve Him with our God-given talents and abilities. Realizing that you are not alone in running your business or following your career, can take away much of the anxiety and burden of managing a business!

Consistently recognizing God's ownership is difficult. It is easy to believe intellectually that God owns all you have and yet live as if it were not true. Here are a number of practical suggestions to help us recognize God's ownership:

For the next 30 days, meditate on 1 Chronicles 29:11,12 when you wake up and just before you go to sleep.

"Yours, O Lord, is the greatness and the power and the glory and the victory and the majesty, for all that is in the heavens and in the earth is yours. Yours is the kingdom, O Lord, and you are exalted as head above all. Both riches and honor come from you, and you rule over all. In your hand are power and might, and in your hand it is to make great and to give strength to all."

Be careful in the use of personal pronouns; consider substituting "the" or "the Lord's for "my," "mine," and "ours."

Ask the Lord to make you aware of His ownership and help you to relinquish ownership. Pray about this over the next 30 days.

Almighty and Sons

When we accept Gods ownership, a new, unique type of company is started. The word company comes from the Latin '*companio*,' meaning "one who eats bread with you." In other words, this company is a partnership with the God who provides. Dennis Peacocke coined the name for this new company "Almighty and Sons", a family business, in his excellent book, "Doing Business God's Way."

As the lead partner, He gives us the necessary resources to develop the business.

He gives financial resources. "So he called ten of his servants and gave them ten minas. 'Put this money to work,' he said, 'until I come back.'" A mina was a Greek monetary unit worth one hundred denarii or about four months' wages for an average worker based on a six-day work week. Quite a large sum, something like $ 80.000!

He gives us skills, intelligence and know-how. "Bezalel and Oholiab and every craftsman in whom the Lord has put skill and intelligence to know how to do any work in the construction of the sanctuary shall work in accordance with all that the Lord has commanded." (Exodus 36:1).

As lead partner, He gives wisdom to make good decisions. "If any of you lacks wisdom, you should ask God, who gives generously to all without finding fault, and it will be given to you." (James 1:5)

As lead partner, he instructs and guides. "The Lord says, "I will guide you along the best pathway for your life.

I will advise you and watch over you. Do not be like a senseless horse or mule that needs a bit and bridle to keep it under control." (Psalm 32:8 nlt)

As lead partner, God is ultimately in control of every event. "We adore you as being in control of everything" (1 Chronicles 29:11, TLB). "The Lord does whatever pleases him, in the heavens and on the earth" (Psalm 135:6). And in the book of Daniel, King Nebuchadnezzar stated: "I praised the Most High; I honored and glorified Him who lives forever.... He does as He pleases with the powers of heaven and the peoples of the earth. No one can hold back His hand or say to him: 'What have you done?'" (Daniel 4:34-35).

As lead partner, God uses even seemingly devastating circumstances for ultimate good in the lives of the godly, whatever the circumstances. "We know that in all things God works for the good of those who love him, who have been called according to his purpose" (Romans 8:28).

Transferring Ownership

Do you remember the last time that you signed over the deed or title of something that you owned? The last time you sold a car, you signed over the car title. When you sold your last house, you signed over the deed at closing. Have you ever sold a business or a commercial property? With a property we may do that quite casually and be glad to get rid of the debt and make some cash. Kent Humphreys tells of the time when, in 1997, he signed over ownership of his distribution firm which his family had owned for 38 years. "It took me about 45 minutes to sign papers on two or three long tables. The next day I was still CEO, but someone else owned the firm. I now had a stewardship position, I still felt responsible and wanted to succeed, but a huge burden was lifted from my shoulders. I was no longer ultimately responsible for the debt, the livelihood of four hundred families, and the final decision. I was accountable to the owner to run it properly." "I remember a meeting of twelve business owners in Kuala Lumpur, Malaysia, in which they signed over the deed to their businesses to Jesus Christ. It was a special privilege for me to be there. Four local pastors were also present. Each company owner read the deed and signed it. The pastors prayed for each business steward individually. Then we prayed, laid hands on the pastors, and commissioned them to be involved in the equipping of each CEO to run their business for Christ. Finally, the pastors prayed for the group of leaders as a whole that their actions would impact the companies, the city, and the nation. We had two witnesses sign each deed and took photos to help remind all involved."

Kent went on to say, "These leaders were involved in the first three groups of 'Fellowship of Companies for Christ' in Malaysia. Each group met for three hours a week. Many of them will now help convene or facilitate another eight-week group or a group that will meet for the next year. Do you realize what an impact this will make on these business leaders? Just as I did in 1997, they assumed the role of CEO as stewards, no longer owners. Every decision must be made in the best interest of the owner, Jesus Christ. They must be obedient stewards and be honest and faithful CEO's. However, Christ is the owner and He will make the final major decisions. That takes the pressure off. All we have to do is submit to His vision, mission, principles, and leadership."

If you feel led to do the same as these Malaysian leaders, just adapt the form below. You can also do this if you do not own a company yourself. In this case you have your career to surrender. I suggest that you have your spouse, pastor, fellow group members, and key employees attend the ceremony. Have witnesses sign the deed with you. Make sure that your peers hold you accountable.

Dedication of the company

I, ………………………………… the legal owner/part-owner of
(Name of the business……………………………………), solemnly declare
before everyone present and before all Heaven and Earth that I on this day
willingly deed the ownership of this company over to the Almighty God,
the creator of all things.
I believe that God, my heavenly Father desires that all things be reconciled
back to Him through His Son Jesus Christ.

As of today, I acknowledge that God is the rightful owner of (Name of
the business…………………………………, and I am merely His steward
looking after His resources.

Therefore, I now repent of all the past wrong doings done by (Name of
the business…………………………………); it's owners, officers and
employees and ask you God to forgive us and cleanse us by the blood of
your son Jesus Christ.

God, I ask you to redeem (Name of the business
………………………………………), all its assets and reputation so
that it can be used to bring glory and honour to your name.

I desire to be a Priest in this company and pledge to lead this company
for Christ to the best of my ability. I will do everything in my capacity
as (Role in the business …………………………………………)
to honour you in all the practices and dealings of (Name of the
business…………………………………)

I now dedicate (Name of the business…………………………………),
all its assets to you for the advancement of your Kingdom.

Help me God to carry out all that I pledge to do, in Jesus name. Amen.

Signed by

………………………………………   ………………………………………
(Name)   (Date)

Witnessed by:

………………………………………   ………………………………………
(Name)   (Date)

DON'T BE SUCH AN ASS!

6

I n 'The Leader of the Future,' Stephen Covey is quoted as saying, "The leaders of the future will be those who create a culture or value system centered upon principles. Creating such a culture in business, government, school, hospital, non-profit organization will be a tremendous and exciting challenge in this new era and will only be achieved by leaders, be they emerging or seasoned, who have the vision, courage and humility to constantly learn and grow. Those people and organizations that have a passion for learning— learning through listening, seeing emerging trends, sensing and anticipating needs in the marketplace, evaluating past successes and mistakes, and absorbing lessons that conscience and principles teach us— to mention just a few ways—will have enduring influence. Such learning leaders will not resist change; they will embrace it."

Stubbornness, and donkeys are surely very hardheaded, forms one of the biggest barriers against learning. Entrepreneurs are also known for this proverbial obstinacy. The Bible offers the possibility to learn from God himself, and it warns against stubbornness, which will only lead to being controlled by another constraining force! Our Big Boss promises, "I will instruct you and teach you in the way you should go; I will counsel you and watch over you." He also warns us about the consequences of not listening to him: "Do not be like the horse or the mule, which have no understanding but must be controlled by bit and bridle or they will not come to you" (Ps. 32:8–9).

To Live is to Learn!

Advice and counsel are essential to the entrepreneur. Seeking and heeding wise and godly counsel enables you to make right decisions in a world more and more interconnected, more and more intertwined with itself, a world in which doing business continues to grow more complex and dynamic, so that constant learning and extra schooling have become a necessity. He who does not learn does not grow, and he who does not grow will die. "The skill of being able to learn quicker than the competitor," Arie de Geus, head of planning at Royal Dutch/Shell tells us, "could be the only benefit that remains for you to keep ahead of the competition."

The ability to learn is an essential skill for a disciple. Indeed, the word disciple, literally means "learner." Jesus invites us to learn from him and he also said, "Everything that I learned from my Father I have made known to you" (John 15:15). Learning starts with listening. And listening is much easier when it's quiet. Take some time this week to really listen to what Jesus wants to tell you. Keeping a quiet time every day, shutting out all sounds and listening intently to Jesus is a very profitable exercise.

A donkey is well known for learning from his experiences, being careful never to make the same mistake twice. Learning from the past is ever so important for Christian entrepreneurs. When you have encountered setbacks or made mistakes, examine what happened, and do all you can to avoid the same circumstances and choices in the future. Socrates said, "The un-examined life is not worth living."

But also bear in mind learning without implementation is only knowledge. "Anyone who listens to the word but does not do what it says is like a man who looks at his face in a mirror and, after looking at himself, goes away and immediately forgets what he looks like. But the man who looks intently into the perfect law that gives freedom, and continues to do this, not forgetting what he has heard, but doing it—he will be blessed in what he does." (James 1:23–25)

In Chapter 10, you can read a description of each decade of my life and which leaders had made the most impact on my life, starting with my grandfather. Looking back on my life in this way was a wonderful exercise, helping me to take inventory of all that has happened to me, so that I could learn from all these experiences.

The Bible contains a story about a talking donkey, which we'll look at in detail in the rest of this chapter. Like Balaam, you too can learn to listen to what your donkey is trying to tell you through your business, assets, career, money, and anything you use to achieve your goal. Our business is a learning school! It is said, that as a man builds a house, the house builds the man! That is certainly true of a business.

What's he telling me now?

Rabbi Moshe needed a donkey for a day or two. He went to Mullah Nasrudin and asked to borrow his donkey. The mullah came with the excuse that he had already lent his donkey to someone else. While he was talking, the donkey started braying loudly in the back yard. Rabbi Moshe looked with an accusing glance at Mullah Nasrudin and told him, "I don't want to have anything to do with you anymore, now that the word of a donkey means more to you than my word!" Our donkey can say things to us which we can learn from!

The whole story of Balaam and his talking donkey can be read in Numbers 22–24. This story, showing clearly God's sense of humor, tells us that Balaam got paid for foretelling the future and the manipulation of people for profit. He accepted that Yahweh, the Lord, was truly a powerful God, but he did not believe that the Lord was the only true God. His heart was taken over by thoughts of the profit he could make in the land of Moab; he saw great potential for growth there. His story shows the deception of pretending to be pious and spiritual while inwardly living a corrupt life. This mixture of wicked motives, pursuit of gain, amorality, and power combined with an outward appearance of the spiritual life ultimately led to his death. What about us? In what ways can we mistreat our donkey; misuse our position, influence, assets, career or business?

The donkey could see something on the road that was invisible to Balaam. An angel wanted to warn him that his strategy was totally wrong. The donkey stood still, and Balaam hit the donkey three times! Later on, the angel of the Lord said to Balaam, "Why have you beaten your donkey these three times? I have come here to oppose you because your path is a reckless one before me. The donkey saw me and turned away from me these three times. If she had not turned away, I would certainly have killed you by now, but I would have spared her" (Num. 22:32–33).

Sometimes God allows certain incidents to happen in our company to warn us. It seems as if the company is saying, "Stop!" What is it that the Lord wants to tell you? How can your company speak to you? Are you willing to listen?

Money, sex and power

I think the three warnings that came directly from the donkey's mouth also have to do with three important aspects of business life: money, sex, and power.

Thomas à Kempis wrote, "It is vanity to strive after honor and a high status. It is vanity to follow the desire of the flesh." Following this statement, monastic orders declared three vows: poverty, chastity, and obedience.

Richard Foster wrote an incredible book called Money, Sex, and Power. In it he described how these three powers, used in the right way, present an enormous opportunity to bring about great blessing in the lives of individuals. But he also warns that these same three items can be turned and used for evil and sinister purposes:

> The demon in money is greed. Nothing can destroy human beings like the passion to possess. The demon of sex is lust. Lust captivates rather than emancipates, devours rather than nourishes. The demon in power is pride. True power desires to set people free, while pride is determined to dominate. True power enhances relationships, pride destroys them.

These three themes were also dealt with by Dostoyevsky in his book 'The Idiot.' Prince Myskin, whom Dostoyevsky portrayed as Christlike, was plunged into the depths of a culture obsessed with money, sex, and power. The people could not fathom what was wrong with the prince, who showed absolutely no vanity, greed, lust, envy, or fear whatsoever. They admired his innocence, but his behavior was so abnormal that they called him the "idiot." Living a Christian life in today's marketplace is just not normal!

What is your donkey saying? Do you hear an inner voice telling you to stop, think, and review your approach? Do you think God wants to step in before you go down too low?

Let's look at these three influences—money, sex, and power—to see the ways in which God can speak to us through our businesses.

Money

"I want to become financially independent" is a common goal among professionals who focus on making a career. Jacques Ellul, as professor of sociology at the University of Bordeaux in France, wrote the following in Money and Power, "When we claim to use money, we make a gross error. We can, if we must, use money, but it is really money that uses us and makes us servants by bringing us under its law and subordinating us to its aims. We are not talking about our inner life; we are observing our total situation. We are not free to direct the use of money one way or another, for we are in the hands of this controlling power, a mode of being, and a form to be used in relating to man."

Balaam, the owner of the donkey, who 'fell in love with the money he could earn by doing wrong,' was very much influenced by his desire for money at all costs. Jude verse 11 (tlb) refers to Balaam, who would "do anything for money." He served the wrong master!

Jesus showed us that money is a trading power, a power able to put things into motion and even able to gain dedication and loyalty! Money in itself is not bad, and it is certainly not sinful to be wealthy.

It can be used for either good or bad. Paul, earning his money as a tentmaker warned us about the dangers of loving money; "But people who long to be rich fall into temptation and are trapped by many foolish and harmful desires that plunge them into ruin and destruction. For the love of money is the root of all kinds of evil. And some people, craving money, have wandered from the true faith and pierced themselves with many sorrows." (1 Tim. 6:9–10 nlt)

Derek Prince, a well-known Bible teacher wrote, "In my teachings I often emphasized God's plan to bless the faithful especially in material things. But looking back I regret every opportunity where I propagated this message of prosperity, without balancing it with Paul's warning."

The second influence, sex, was also no stranger to Balaam.

Sex

"You cannot stop birds from flying over your head, but you can make sure they do not build a nest in your hair." This quote can be applied to keeping out of the trap of unbridled sexuality. I can now thank God when I see a beautiful girl. But seeing is not looking, and looking is not watching, which could lead to action, as King David discovered. I must admit, though, that I do feel a little safer now that I am in my late sixties. I feel as though I am like a dog chasing a car. If he caught it, he just wouldn't know what to do with it!

"I sit behind my desk for hours on end. My job is so boring. It takes a lot of effort to keep my mind on the job at the time just crawls by. Were it not for the beautiful women who work in our office, who make me think about sex and distract my mind, I think I'd go crazy." This quotation comes from psychiatrist Archibald Hart's book 'The Crazy-Making Workplace' and voices the experience of many people. Sexual longings are a powerful force in men and in women.

Balaam misused this force toward his own ends, and his talking donkey tried to restrain him from it. In his ambition to put his stamp on society, Balaam enticed the children of Israel to eat food sacrificed to idols and to commit sexual sin (see Rev. 2:14). Sexuality is irrevocably combined with worship, and when we get married, we promise to honor one another physically: "With my body, I thee worship."

In their immorality the Israelites started to "indulge in sexual immorality with Moabite women, who invited them to the sacrifices to their gods" (Num. 25:1–2). Balaam used unnatural sexuality as a method to get the people back into slavery again. "And the Lord opened the mouth of the donkey" (Num. 22:28).

Money and sex are used in all sorts of markets as powerful instruments to get us under the yoke of false gods who are determined to manipulate us and lay claim to our loyalty. Pornography is unnatural and dishonorable; real art is noble and therefore uplifting. It seems tempting to step into a dream world, but it is deceitful and misleading. Lust is like a bolting stallion, an uncontrollable sexual passion, which only pursues to possess. Richard Foster stated, "When from a feeling of excitement the plan develops to use someone, when attraction degenerates into intrigues, then we have already overstepped the boundary between excitement and spiritual adultery." Sexism in the workplace is the urge to dominate or to manipulate the other person.

Karl Barth was the first theologian who declared that human sexuality is based on the 'Imago Dei,' the image of God. The core of our identity is formed by relationships, because we are created after God's image. Sexuality and spirituality are not supposed to be each other's enemies, but each other's friends. What is the key? The key is fidelity! Emil Brunner said, "Fidelity is the ethical element that strengthens natural love." One of the most successful entrepreneurs in the Bible, Job, illustrates this as follows: "I made a covenant with my eyes not to look lustfully at a girl" (Job 31:1).

The wedding vows are, of course, very well known. Unfortunately, today's businesspeople have the means and opportunity to indulge in satisfying their sexual appetites. I remember visiting a conference in St. Louis, Missouri, some years ago. The hotel manager sadly told us that during a previous conference of Christian businesspeople, he witnessed the all-time heaviest use of in-room adult film viewing in his tenure at the hotel.

I recently read a confession of guilt from the mayor of the town next to mine. During a difficult period in his marriage he visited a brothel. This came out and was exaggerated in the press. As a Christian he has talked and worked this through with his wife and also publicly asked forgiveness. Faithfulness means keeping your covenant with God, with your wife, and with the people around you.

An important verse in my life has been Proverbs 5:18: "May your fountain be blessed, and may you rejoice in the wife of your youth." I have claimed this promise from God many times, and I thank God for more than foty-five years of marriage to my wife; which speaks to her strength of character more than mine!

Power

"If he is a Christian, then please count me out." In a previous chapter I mentioned the scenario where I heard these words, but they bear repeating. One of the main objections against the good news of Jesus Christ is perceptible hypocrisy, the misuse of spirituality for gain. Balaam's donkey warned him to stop and think about what he was doing. The angel said to Balaam, "Three times the donkey saw me and shied away" (Num. 22:33 nlt).

The third reason for the donkey contradicting Balaam, is the misuse of spirituality, "having a form of godliness but denying its power" (2 Tim. 3:5).

In Numbers 22–24, Balaam demonstrates how well he, as a prophet, could appraise trends and predict the future. He even predicted the star of Bethlehem (see Num. 24:17). He would have been a very popular guy at the annual meetings of the World Economic Forum in Davos, Switzerland. He would have had the gift of getting insight into God's handling of the world. Futurists and people who can predict trends are doing good business these days. At a prominent Dutch management institute, one can even take a course in 'business astrology.' At the end of the course the participants have a business plan according to the stars! Balaam had no idea about the difference between spiritual gifts and spiritual fruits.

Having received a spiritual gift means that we have the ability to do something, but spiritual fruit develops from character. A gift is given; bearing fruit comes from a slow process of character forming. Our businessman Balaam impressed the local king very much with his insights. He had a spiritual gift, but he could not bear spiritual fruit! This king knew what he wanted to hear from Balaam, so he made Balaam a proposal he could not refuse.

I was struck by the honesty of a leader of a multinational bank when he said, "We are not interested in the development of business ethics on the basis of altruism, but we do it just because it is good business." Fair enough—honest, but misled. "An ethical entrepreneur does not exist," according to the former Dutch prime minister Ruud Lubbers in 2000. "The only reason we act responsibly is that the both the press and public opinion will play it up if we don't." I am aware that reporters sometimes misinterpret quotations, but these words from the former prime minister and leader of the Christian Democrat party voice the sentiments of many. Honesty at last!

To tie the donkey (enterprise, venture, business, career) to the vine means to bear fruit. Jesus said, "If a man remains in me and I in him, he will bear much fruit; apart from me you can do nothing" (John 15:5). Only by remaining in constant contact with the True Vine can we ever bear true, satisfying spiritual fruit. Fruit is the ultimate test of the vitality of spiritual life, and the fruit of the Spirit is "love, joy, peace, patience, kindness, goodness, faithfulness, gentleness and self-control" (Gal. 5:22–23). This is true power, and these qualities are much needed in the marketplace. But unfortunately, the opposite is often demonstrated, as with Balaam; "People will love only themselves and their money. They will be boastful and proud, scoffing at God, disobedient to their parents, and ungrateful. They will consider nothing sacred. They will be unloving and unforgiving; they will slander others and have no self-control. They will be cruel and hate what is good. They will betray their friends, be reckless, be puffed up with pride, and love pleasure rather than God. They will act religious, but they will reject the power that could make them godly." (2 Tim. 3:2–5 nlt)

Regrettably this is what we often encounter in the marketplace. Balaam wanted to experience who God is, but his motivation was totally wrong. He used religion for his own purposes. The end he longed for was very clear to him: "Let me die like the righteous; let my life end like theirs" (Num. 23:10 nlt). His prayers were not answered. He was executed together with the Moabites whose money tempted him to join them against God.

Turn, turn, turn

In Numbers 22:22 we read that the angel of the Lord stood in the road to oppose Balaam. If there is one thing we as Chris- tian entrepreneurs do not want, then this is it: being opposed by an angel of the Lord! Balaam ignored God's warnings, but the donkey didn't. The donkey turned off the road three times, preventing Balaam from continuing his planned journey.

The first warning came when the donkey saw the angel and turned off the road into a field. Balaam beat her in an attempt to get her back on track. He knew his enterprise was not on the right track. He had to be deviated from his plan, making him restless and wanting to get back on course. Could this be a warning to your company? Are disappointing results forcing to go in a direction you do not want to go? Have you landed in a new market area you really do not want to be in? Do you think this could be a warning sign?

The second warning came on a narrow track in between the vineyards, with a wall on both sides. The donkey was afraid when he saw the angel and pressed close to the wall, crushing Balaam's foot against it. That must have hurt! Balaam's enterprise was painful for him. Is your company hurting you? Physically maybe? Headaches, high blood pressure, too much stress, burnout? Frustrations because of conflicts and lack of motivation? Could this be a warning from God?

The third warning came because the angel stood in a narrow place where there was no room to turn at all, either to the right or to the left. The donkey lay down, with Balaam still on her back, and he beat her again. There was no way at all for Balaam's enterprise to go. He was at his wits' end and took his sword to kill the animal. Has your business come to a deadlock? No more liquidity? Stagnation of the market? Is the bank pulling the plug out, and is the cash flowing like a rushing river? A contract ended? What does God want to tell you?

The Bible warns us, "It is a terrible thing to fall into the hands of the living God" (Heb. 10:31 nlt). Let us heed the warning given by the Apostle Peter who wrote, ""They have gone off the road and become like Balaam, son of Beor, who fell in love with the money he could make by doing wrong. And Balaam was stopped from his mad course when his donkey spoke to him with a human voice, scolding and rebuking him" (2 Peter 2:15.16).

Experiencing a roadblock in your business? Os Hillman wrote about donkey business in one of his excellent daily meditations. "There are times when pushing harder, trying to manipulate the circumstance, or pressing those around you is not the response to have to the road-block. God may be trying to have you reconsider your ways. God may be doing one of four things when you are faced with an obstacle:

- He's blocking it to protect you.

- His timing to complete a certain phase of plans is not the same as yours, and He may need you to first go through a process of character refinement.

- He may want other players to get in place, and the circumstances are not yet ready for them to enter.

- He may be using the process to develop patience in you. Relying on the Holy Spirit to know which one applies to your situation is the key to moving in God's timing.

A donkey has big ears. Learn to use them to listen to what God is telling you!

DONKEY FRUIT

7

"You did not choose me, but I chose you and appointed you to go and bear fruit—fruit that will last. Then the Father will give you whatever you ask in my name." (John 15:16).

The ultimate outcome of the fruit of a Christian's business is to bring honor and glory to God. It is all about God's reputation. People will watch how you do business, how you work, how you relate to your employees, how you deal with debt, how you tackle difficulties. The goal is that when they see you working, they see Jesus in action and then say, "There must be something to that faith in God!" Jesus challenged his followers: "Let your light shine before men, that they may see your good deeds and praise your Father in heaven" (Matt. 5:16).

Like the donkey who carried Jesus into Jerusalem on Palm Sunday, the business becomes a "Jesus bearer" to bring him where he wants to be, to do what he intends to do. Real success in business is when God's name and reputation are held high by the company and enlarged in the eyes of everybody that company influences.

The apostle Paul had something to say about bearing fruit. "God is the one who provides seed for the farmer and then bread to eat. In the same way, he will provide and increase your resources and then produce a great harvest of generosity in you. Yes, you will be enriched in every way so that you can always be generous. And when we take your gifts to those who need them, they will thank God" (2 Cor. 9:10–11 nlt). This agricultural metaphor gives us insight into six areas in which our business bears fruit, like the six points of a Star of David, letting God's light shine for the people who live in the dark. These six areas are as follows:

- Increasing the assets of the company
  —"God … will increase your resources."

- Meeting needs of those in the business
  —"God … provides … bread to eat."

- Creating products to serve others
  —"God … provides seed."

- Cultivating integrity in the way we do business
  —"he will … produce a great harvest of generosity."

- Investing in God's work
  —"you can always be generous."

- Witnessing to God's work among us
  —"they will thank God."

Let's look at each one of these in more detail.

Increasing the assets of the company

To start with, the company has to have assets. Seed has to be sown, and no profit has been made yet. Too often our first trip is to go to the bank to ask for starting capital. Not that this is a wrong move, but considering that God gives the sower seed, could we possibly first ask him to lead us to the source of capital? Maybe he has other ideas!

My friend Simon came back to Holland after an American adventure, during which he went bankrupt, got divorced from his wife, and suffered a period of extreme psychological breakdown. While recovering, he became a Christian. Back in Holland he wanted to start all over again as an entrepreneur, but this time together with the Lord. He didn't have a penny to his name and wondered how he could get startup capital. He went on a three-day retreat to a monastery to pray. Shortly thereafter, his former partner in the US business phoned and offered him the chance to take over some Dutch customers of the American company. Apparently, it was too difficult for the American company to serve those customers well because of the distance, but they were of high potential. Simon could take over these clients against a commission on the future turnover. After he spoke with the clients, they even offered to pay part of the contract in advance. That gave Simon the much-needed financial breathing space. Seven years later, the business is consolidated, and Simon needs the bank only for a small amount of credit in current account. The credit is also completely guaranteed by the receivables balance. He is determined to remain debt free!

Do you think that God can provide starting capital without borrowing?

Profit is essential for the continuity of the company, to build up capital, ensuring seed for next year. Nothing makes a bigger contribution to the financial freedom of the company than building up enough assets, so that a business has sufficient cash flow to finance all the work. The entrepreneur can then also survive during bad times and invest during good times. Building up assets is a gift from God; he can and will provide! "But remember the Lord your God, for it is he who gives you the ability to produce wealth, and so confirms his covenant, which he swore to your forefathers, as it is today" (Deut. 8:18). Profit must never be the purpose of the company, but it is certainly necessary for the continuation of the business.

Meeting needs of those involved in the business

The entrepreneur has the privilege to provide for the income of everybody involved with the company. Co-workers and their families depend on the company for their daily needs. To pay an honest salary, on time, is a fruit of the enterprise.

Here again the Lord God promises to provide sufficiently for our daily bread, and a prayer for this fits very well in the daily consultation between the entrepreneur and his heavenly Father. "Give is this day, our daily bread!" Responsibility for the supply of income for families does not stop with your own employees. It reaches further too! The business also bears responsibility for the income of the people supplying the company with products or services. It is essential to pay on time and completely. "The Lord asked, 'Who then is the faithful and wise manager, whom the master puts in charge of his servants to give them their food allowance at the proper time?" (Luke 12:42).

The Bible says that complaints from creditors about those who don't pay fully and on time reach the ears of the Lord himself, and withholding payments are a reason for God to take action! "Look! The wages you failed to pay the workmen who mowed your fields are crying out against you. The cries of the harvesters have reached the ears of the Lord Almighty." (James 5:4). One of the highest priorities of the company that glorifies God is to fulfill their obligations in time.

In my workshops for business people, I like to ask the question, "Who is your best customer?" Of course, it is the customer who pays on time! So when an entrepreneur tells the supplier, "I will pay within thirty days," but he does not pay until forty-five, sixty days or longer without informing the supplier, then he has misled his creditor and lied to him. Remember that you are tied to the Vine, in partnership with the Lord Jesus, and by not keeping your word you are pulling the Lord Jesus down with you as well, involving the Lord in an act of deceitfulness. "God is not a man, that he should lie, nor a son of man, that he should change his mind. Does he speak and then not act? Does he promise and not fulfill?" (Num. 23:19).

To pay on time means that your co-workers are stress-free and content, and that your suppliers like to do business with you. I remember the time when I was director of a chemical specialty company in the 1970s, when the oil crisis was at its height. It was hard to get raw materials. Fortunately, we had a good reputation with our suppliers because we'd always paid our invoices on time. During the shortage, our supplier came to me and offered preferential treatment when they had to ration the raw materials because, he said, "Your company always paid their invoices on time, so you get first deliveries."

Creating products to serve others

The entrepreneur uses his raw materials—in our metaphor, the seed—and his God-given talents and skills to see the seed germinate and multiply to produce many ears of corn, followed by further processing or by taking to the marketplace for sale. Naturally he cares for the environment and guards the production process, so as to guarantee the quality. In our agricultural example, the farmer is dependent on many factors out of his control, such as weather conditions, wind and rain, and market factors.

Many farmers profess their dependence on God in this way. In the same way the Christian entrepreneur is very much dependent on the blessing of the Lord in his work. Bill, a friend of mine and the owner of a company in the building trade always told me, "It doesn't matter how hard you work. You can work until you're exhausted but earn nothing. Then suddenly something might happen, or a new customer comes your way, or you get a brilliant idea, get 'lucky,' and you're successful." He liked to quote his favorite Bible text: "The blessing of the Lord brings wealth, and he adds no trouble to it" (Prov. 10:22).

Our God is Lord of all physical, chemical, biological, and cognitive processes. Would he not help both the farmer and the businessperson by finding solutions for technical, marketing, or financial problems? A company tied to the vine is assured of the indwelling creativity of the Creator who made it all. Many times I prayed not only for the inter-relational aspects of our work but also for technical and financial problems.

Gunnar Olson from Sweden, an exceptional man whom I admire and respect very much, is the founder of ICCC, the International Christian Chamber of Commerce. He tells of a time in which he was experiencing great difficulties in his plastics factory with an extruder. After months of problems and finally coming to his wits' end, he and some of his co-workers started to pray for a solution to this problem. They gathered around the machine, put their hands on it, and prayed, asking the Lord to help them. The folllwing day, they received the solution from an unexpected source, and it turned out to be very simple. One vital part was utilized wrongly. A new component was machined, installed in a different way, and the extruder worked perfectly again.

In my workshops, I tell the story of the very first product which man made. You can read about it in Genesis 3. Adam and Eve suddenly found themselves expelled from the garden in a totally new, strange envoironment. They discovered that they were naked and set about rectifying this problem. They made clothes out of fig leaves. Now, this was not very smart. Such garments would tear easily and were not so attractive. Moreover, the fig leaves were rough leaving them with itches. The clothes were cold in the winter and may not have covered all the strategically important places. God was watching them and ecided to come up with his own product. Fur coats! Durable and beautiful, cool in the summer, warm in winter. They adequately covered all necessary body parts. God even 'clothed them,' giving the idea of individual tailoring! Now that's better! I am convinced that God will also look at your product or service and show you how to make a product which truly meets needs!

Cultivating integrity in the way we do business

The Bible says, God will "enlarge the harvest of your righteousness" (2 Cor. 9:10).

A common experience of the Christian entrepreneur seems to be an inherent inability to do what is right. Nothing the great apostle Paul experienced is alien to us. "I do not understand what I do. For what I want to do, I do not do, but what I hate, I do. And if I do what I do not want to do, I agree that the law is good. As it is, it is no longer I myself who do it, but it is sin living in me. I know that nothing good lives in me, that is, in my sinful nature. For I have the desire to do what is good, but I cannot carry it out. For what I do is not the good I want to do; no, the evil I do not want to do—this I keep on doing.

Now if I do what I do not want to do, it is no longer I who do it, but it is sin living in me that does it." (Rom. 7:15–20)

When you are tied to the vine Christ's life can flow through you to bring to light a life of righteousness, a life of living in a right relationship to God, the ability to do what is right! That really sums up a donkey business; it's a transaction—your life for the life of Christ! His life flows through yours to bear fruit. That's the best deal there is!

Robert, a friend of mine, owns a company that buys up old stock-lots of end-of-line cosmetics to sell to large chain stores. "In my business," he said, "it's quite normal to lie about the origin and production dates of these products. But now that I consciously do business with God, I notice that I've stopped telling lies. For the first time I realized that the commandment, 'you shall not lie' is not really a commandment, but a promise for anyone doing business with God. It's like God saying, 'When you follow me you won't have to lie!' The liberating effect of all this is that when a customer phones me, I don't have to think about what I told him the last time!"

A recent study by Professor Johann Graafland, professor of economy, business, and ethics at the University of Tilburg, Netherlands, showed that experienced entrepreneurs who believe in God say they experience more dilemmas than those who do not follow any belief system. This comes from a sharpening of our conscience, being tied to the vine, by the indwelling Holy Spirit of God, so that you receive a deeper sense of sin. That same Spirit bears this fruit in us, and in our company. Integrity means Christ's life is revealed through us as we go about our daily business. "He must become greater; I must become less" (John 3:30).

Investing in God's Work

During the process of doing business together with God, Paul continued to say, "You will be made rich in every way so that you can be generous on every occasion, and … your generosity will result in thanksgiving to God" (2 Cor. 9:11).

In the agricultural economy in Old Testament times, it was the duty of the Jewish entrepreneur to give the firstfruits of his labor to God. When you realize that you have assumed the position of a steward and no longer the owner of the company, that you are now the manager of the assets of God's business, it becomes logical that the new owner will want to use part of his wealth for his own purposes.

"Honor the Lord with your wealth, with the first fruits of all your crops; then your barns will be filled to overflowing, and your vats will brim over with new wine" (Prov. 3:9–10). This relates to giving a tenth part of the increase of your assets from one year to another, determined at the harvest time. The easiest calculation method is to give a tenth of the profits of the business, representing the increase in assets. Reserving a tenth of the increase in your assets is a basic condition for God's blessing, without even speaking about sacrificial giving. In order to ensure that a tenth of the profit would flow to God's kingdom, Bert, a friend of mine, transferred 10 percent of the shares of his company to a trust. This way he prevents any discussions about it and even if he sells the company, God's tenth part of the profits is guaranteed. On top of that he explores other possibilities to use his assets, making these available for the use of the kingdom. His office facilities are available for the local Christian community, he sponsors impoverished children, helps co-workers who have special problems, and so forth. Together with his advisers and fellow entrepreneurs he constantly looks for other possibilities to devote more of the assets of the company toward God's goals.

Witnessing to God's work among us

Our theme verse for this chapter, 2 Corinthians 9:11 goes on to say that all this "results in thanksgiving to God." This is what doing business is all about. Ultimately God must be glorified, uplifted, and receive all honor. People in and around the business should know and see that God is actively involved with the believing CEO and his or her work. God is not distant; he wants to be very close and longs for a relationship with all people. We have to make sure that everything we do corresponds with what we say. It must be evident from our words and deeds that we are Christians.

The most powerful testimony shines through in hard times. The Christian CEO lives in a kind of glass house and his responses and reactions are constantly being observed from all sides, especially during setbacks. And it is precisely during such times that the true character reveals itself. Co-workers and customers watch how you react when you make mistakes, or when you are faced with your own limitations, or when you are deceived in the market. Do you react in a godly way, commensurate with the name you carry as a Christian?

WWJD—What Would Jesus Do?—will be your first prayer in such circumstances, and you will perceive that the life of Jesus flows through the vine and the donkey to reveal itself. This enables us to dare to be vulnerable, to make the proper decisions, and to do what is good. Our goal is for God's name, his reputation, to be enhanced and upheld so that others can see it.

But it is not enough only to do the right thing, deal ethically, love your neighbor, and so forth. At a certain time you have to confess with your mouth that you trust God for the suc- cess of your company and expect everything from him. Jesus gave a powerful promise and warning: "Whoever acknowledges me before men, I will also acknowledge him before my Father in heaven. But whoever disowns me before men, I will disown him before my Father in heaven" (Matt. 10:32–33). When we acknowledge and confess Jesus, then he will represent us and our case at the throne of the Father. What a partner to have!

I remember looking and praying for ways to witness to our employees and customers at the European Space Agency. Every month, we held a lunch for our employees who were working on loan at the Space Agency, and it was our custom to say a prayer of thanksgiving prior to the meal. Some employees appreciated it, some did not care and others hated it. Once, a national newspaper interviewed me about my faith and how it applied to our company's affairs. I told the journalist that our company "belonged to God" and that we prayed for employees and customers by name regularly. The article was published, and that same day, I received a call from the chair of our workers' council, complaining that this would cost us contracts and jobs if we didn't stop professing to our faith in God. (This was at the same time our contracts were being renewed as explained in an earlier chapter.) He asked me to attend a meeting of all the employees to explain what I meant. This was a major opportunity to witness to all. Then I discovered that the PR office of the space agency had found the article on the Web and sent a clipping to all the managers! I was called before a French contracts officer, who had taken offense at an interview that had appeared in a Dutch newspaper in which I had witnessed to the fact that we ran our business according to biblical principles and prayed at the agency. The article mentioned us "praying in a space lab." The officer said that such utterances, if spoken in France would get us hauled into court for using religion in a public institution. The word got out—all over the Space Agency!

Paul admonished us to "preach the word at all times: whether it is convenient or not! If we don't do it voluntarily, we may be forced to. I experienced that the Lord honored this testimony. Our contracts position did not suffer at all.

Triple bottom line

Pete Ochs, the founder of Capital III, is an entrepreneur with manufacturing, real estate, energy, and education companies in the US and Latin America. Pete named the company Capital III because of his conviction that businesses should have a triple bottom line: economic, social, and spiritual. The economic bottom line is created by operating a profitable enterprise. The social bottom line occurs when the business leverages its financial resources to creatively meet social needs. And the spiritual bottom line materializes when the company intentionally uses its platform to influence its employees, vendors, and customers for Christ.

Pete realized that the glue to ensure the businesses would remain focused on accomplishing the triple bottom line were Capital III's Vision, Mission, and Values:

Our Vision is to help change the world through entrepreneurship. Our Mission is to be an absolutely trusted business. Our Values are to honour God by serving people, pursuing excellence, and stewarding resources.

In 2009, Capital III bought a bankrupt manufacturing business located in a small rural community. Their biggest dilemma was how to hire enough workers in a town with a very small labor force. To compound the problem, they needed employees that would work a completely flexible schedule - from 20 to 40 hours a week - depending entirely on the volume of business.

Pete and his leadership team prayed and sought the Lord's direction. They were led to try something completely out of the box. They approached the local state-operated correctional facility about utilizing the prison population as the labour force. Inmates were earning only about 70 cents an hour, and Capital III could pay them a starting salary of about $10 an hour. Approximately thirty percent of their wage would be used to reimburse the state for their room and board. The rest they could spend, save, or send to help support their families.

This creative solution has accomplished all three bottom lines.

Economic: Because the labor force is flexible, the company is able to control and reduce its labor costs, meet the just-in-time demands of its customers, and reduce inventories, all of which contribute to the profitability of the business. The company also doesn't need to compensate the work force with paid vacation time! Inmates can earn up to $100 per day, compared to $7 while working for the state.

Social: The state and taxpayers benefit because a portion of what the prisoners earn defrays the cost of room and board. Prisoners are motivated to behave well while in prison, because anyone involved with a disciplinary problem is not eligible to work for Capital III. The prisoners also learn marketable skills that will help them earn a living once they are released from prison. Interestingly, the inmates have chosen to send a majority of what they receive in salary to help support their families.

Spiritual: Capital III is committed to treating the work force with respect and to help them in practical ways. They are helping to build a spiritual life center at the prison, in which

life skill classes and Bible studies are conducted. Capital III also has been instrumental in starting a seminary inside the prison. The business also provides periodic meals and get-togethers for the workers and their families. Every two weeks, Capital III provides motivational and inspirational programs for its workers. In short, the workers have been valued and loved. This has influenced many to consider Christ as their Savior.

Pete Ochs has a big vision. He is praying for the Lord to replicate this model of valuing people and creating economic, social, and spiritual capital in businesses across America and around the world.

DONKEY FODDER

8

"The ox knows his master, the donkey his owner's manger, but Israel does not know, my people do not understand." (Isaiah 1:3). In contrast to the ox, a somewhat slavish animal that makes itself dependent on its owner, the donkey is more of a pig-headed creature well known for going about its own way. But he is by no means stupid. Matthew Henry wrote in his commentary about Isaiah 1:3, "The ass has such a sense of interest as to know his master's crib, where he is fed, and to abide by it." He knows where it is good to be and he loves his food!

Watch Your Weight

Jim, an Irish friend of mine, owns two donkeys. He has to monitor the animals' diet to make sure they don't gain too much weight. An overweight donkey will lie down, roll over onto his back, and be unable to get up again. He then becomes unfit for use. How can a company become too fat?

In this regard, I had to think about Jesus' parable of the rich fool. "The ground of a certain rich man produced a good crop. He thought to himself, "What shall I do? I have no place to store my crops." Then he said, "This is what I'll do. I will tear down my barns and build bigger ones, and there I will store all my grain and my goods. And I'll say to myself, 'You have plenty of good things laid up for many years. Take life easy; eat, drink and be merry.'" But God said to him, "You fool! This very night your life will be demanded from you. Then who will get what you have prepared for yourself?" This is how it will be with anyone who stores up things for himself but is not rich toward God. (Luke 12:15–21)

Beware of success—its upkeep can mean your downfall! Becoming proud with your wealth, telling yourself "you have plenty of good things laid up for many years" means you are not depending on God. God warn us in Deuteronomy 8:17–18 not to say, "My power and the strength of my hands have produced this wealth for me," but rather to realize that "it is the Lord your God … who gives you power to create wealth, and so confirms his covenant, which he swore to your forefathers, as it is today."

To increase profits and assets can never be a goal in itself, nor can wealth be used upon which to base your security. The goal of capital gains, as it is stated in Deuteronomy, is to affirm the relationship with God; also between God and man, and between man and God. Is your wealth being used for God's purposes? Take care, pride will always come before a fall!

Hoarding money makes a company fat and useless to the kingdom of God. Financial freedom does not mean that you have enough assets to live a quiet life, but that you acknowledge God as being the source of everything you will ever need. Dependence on God also means independence from money. You then see money as a means, and not an end. Our donkey must not become a golden calf!

Salted Fodder

What sort of food are we going to give our donkeys? A donkey that is tied to the vine first of all needs salted food. "He will also give you rain for the seed you will sow in the ground, and bread from the yield of the ground, and it will be rich and plenteous; on that day your livestock will graze in a roomy pasture. Also the oxen and the donkeys which work the soil will eat salted fodder, which has been winnowed with shovel and fork" (Isa. 30:23–24 nasb).

Why salted food? To get a glimpse of its meaning we have to look at a picture illustrated in the Old Testament. And we read this in 2 Kings 2:19: "The men of the city said to Elisha, 'Look, our lord, this town is well situated, as you can see, but the water is bad and the land is unproductive.'" Here we have a picture of a beautiful city, nicely situated. Merchants loved to come to this town and spend a few days there. And yet, behind this impressive appearance lies sorrow among the inhabitants; there is a large burden on the shoulders of the people who live and work there. Despite the visibly beautiful surroundings, despite the appreciation of its visitors, the inhabitants are weighed down by an inner secret. The drinking water is bad and the soil causes plants to sprout and then die. The water is foul, but it does not mean that there is no water at all, but that the water is stagnant and brings forth infertility.

Despite the fact that the soil brought about infertility, there surely was some growth. You could see the beginning of harvest, small shoots coming up from the earth, full of promise. The trees were bearing blossom with the promise of an abundant harvest. It all looked so good! Herein lies the tragedy of the city. Ultimately there was no harvest. Maybe in the hearts of the farmers there was always the desire that it would be better next year. After all, they had been working hard and used all their talents to make sure that next year everything would be different, but deep, deep down they knew, "no, it is still not going to work this time; we know exactly what is going to happen." And that is what happened. The fruit fell to the ground, even before it started to ripen to be harvested, so that it again became useless.

Is this a picture of your business? It may look all right, and perhaps people speak highly of the way everything is organized and are impressed by the know-how found in the company. The products initially look fine, the co-workers are well qualified, and the suppliers are pleased with such a customer. But something is wrong, problems arise with customers, and it becomes difficult to find the cause. Customers cancel orders and start to claim; quarrels arise between sales and production workers; it becomes more difficult to pay the suppliers. Pressure rises, you keep plodding on, but you do not seem to succeed. It looks as if there is no blessing on your work.

A way out can be found by tying your donkey to the vine and giving him salted fodder. Let's continue with our picture from 2 Kings 2. Look at verses 20–22:

"Bring me a new bowl," he said, "and put salt in it." So they brought it to him. Then he went out to the spring and threw the salt into it, saying, "This is what the Lord says: 'I have healed this water. Never again will it cause death or make the land unproductive.'" And the water has remained wholesome to this day, according to the word Elisha had spoken."

Salt is a picture of the resurrection power of the glorified Redeemer, given to Christians by the indwelling Holy Spirit. This power, the life of Jesus himself, flows through the vine, through the donkey to bear fruit. As a Christian entrepreneur, you are now a member of "a holy priesthood, offering spiritual sacrifices acceptable to God through Jesus Christ" (1 Peter 2:5). It is Jesus himself who makes our sacrifices pleasing to God. It is only his activity through you that deserves his approval. And what about salt? "Season all your grain offerings with salt. Do not leave the salt of the covenant of your God out of your grain offerings; add salt to all your offerings" (Lev. 2:13). Under no circumstances, God told Moses, should offerings be brought without making them tasty with salt. Without salt, sacrifices are not acceptable, despite all our good intentions.

In Luke 14:33, Jesus told us the minimum requirements for discipleship: "Any of you who does not give up everything he has cannot be my disciple." This is the sacrifice the law demands from us. To give up all that we own is a minimal requirement! Jesus continued in verses 34–35: "Salt is good, but if it loses its saltiness, how can it be made salty again? It is fit neither for the soil nor for the manure pile; it is thrown out. He who has ears to hear, let him hear." Jesus called Christians the "salt of the earth." Our complete surrender to God is what gives salt in food its pleasant taste, and in exchange God gives us a complete indwelling of his Spirit. Being called the salt of the earth does not derive from our own activity, but from the activity of the life of Jesus through us.

He has to be the source of all we do, the first person we consult. Leviticus 2:13 speaks about the "salt of the covenant." This is God's promise of power given to whoever enters into a covenant with him. Salt has to be added to the fodder! Salt must be added right at the source to make the water healthy and life giving. That salt stands for the bond with Jesus, tying your donkey to the vine!

Donkey problems

A farmer's donkey fell into a deep well. No matter how hard he tried, there was no way the farmer could pull his donkey out of the pit. Eventually, he decided to fill up the well with soil and rubble so as to bury the donkey under the rubbish. Together with some friends he carted wheelbarrows full of soil and rubbish and threw it into the pit to bury the donkey. While he was doing that, the donkey stepped on top of each new load of earth, and finally managed to step out of the well by himself!

In this chapter we talk about donkey fodder. An important part of the donkey's diet is formed by the food of problems! We, as entrepreneurs, are problem solvers! Sometimes this can be merely tiring. Other times, we are at our wits' end, not being able to cope with the multiple problems piling up on our desks, and feel almost devoured by them.

When spying out the Promised Land prior to entering Canaan, the spies did their utmost to convince the Israelites about the seemingly insurmountable problems involved in taking possession of the Promised Land. Ten of the spies said, "The land we explored devours those living in it. All the people we saw there are of great size. We saw the Nephilim there.… We seemed like grasshoppers in our own eyes, and we looked the same to them" (Num. 13:32–33).

Joshua and Caleb, however, advised the people, "Do not be afraid of the people of the land, because we will swallow them up. Their protection is gone, but the Lord is with us. Do not be afraid of them" (Num. 14:9). "We will swallow them up." Problems? We'll swallow them whole! Quite often it is the shadow cast before a problem that makes us fearful. Faith means that the Lord is with us, so the shadow fades under the light God shines on the problem.

- What lessons can we learn from the story of the donkey in the well?

- When you are in a hole there is always a way out.

- Stay focused on the outcome even when more problems seem to occur.

- Problems stacked on top of each other may bring the solution.

- Don't give up, even when you can't find a solution.

- Stay optimistic!

To be in business with the Lord means that we must learn to cope with difficulties in the market and the business itself. To be in business with the Lord first of all means trusting God for the results. Peter wrote, "Dear friends, do not be surprised at the painful trial you are suffering, as though something strange were happening to you. But rejoice that you participate in the sufferings of Christ, so that you may be overjoyed when his glory is revealed" (1 Peter 4:12–13).

The first thing we have to do when problems arise is to thank the Lord—under all circumstances. To thank God for problems, means that we realize that he will also take care of the outcome. The solution will surely amaze us! To be in business with the Lord means realizing that difficulties bring opportunities.

Paul decided to stay in the town of Ephesus despite heavy conflicts, "because a great door for effective work has opened to me, and there are many who oppose me" (1 Cor. 16:9). To be in business with the Lord means cultivating perseverance, as Paul experienced when he wrote, "We also rejoice in our sufferings, because we know that suffering produces perseverance; perseverance, character; and character, hope. And hope does not disappoint us, because God has poured out his love into our hearts by the Holy Spirit, whom he has given us" (Rom. 5:3–5).

Keep on top of the business

Businesses are like kids. When you're not watching them, they get up to all sorts of mischief! Donkeys need to be well looked after and managed; so do businesses.

Once upon a time . . . a donkey thought he was very clever. Every day, his master harnessed him to a cart loaded with goods. They always went the same way to the village: along a wide path through the wood, down a gentle slope into farmland, then along the river to the ford and over the plain to the village.

Since the route was always the same, the donkey's master had got into the habit of having a snooze on top of the cart while the donkey, who knew the way by heart plodded on.

Feeling unwell one day, the man decided to risk sending the donkey by himself with a load for urgent delivery. When the animal returned, he was given a double ration of oats as reward.

"Since you're so clever at remembering the way," the man said, "I'm going to send you alone always, then I can do other jobs!" And from then on, in all kinds of weather, the donkey travelled to the village by himself. His master was delighted.

However, one morning, when the donkey reached the river, he decided to shorten his journey by wading across the water. But he entered the river at a deep spot, much deeper than the donkey expected, and he had to swim against the current.

Luckily, he was carrying a load of salt hay, and some of it dissolved in the water, easing the donkey's load, so that he reached the other side without much difficulty. "I am clever," said the donkey, pleased with himself. "I've found a short cut."

Next day, the man loaded the cart with sponges, and the donkey set off as usual. When he arrived at the river, he again thought he would take the short cut, and entered the water as he had done the day before. But this time, the sponges soaked up the water and made the cart heavy, so that the poor animal could not keep his head above water. And in spite of all his efforts, the donkey that thought he was so clever, sank below the surface of the water together with his load.

Don't neglect your business!

Evaluating your financial health (both corporate and personal) is absolutely vital in helping you make the best possible decisions for growth and diagnosing your financial situation. I often see business owners neglecting their finances, and only attending to them when it five to twelve. Your numbers are the number one indicator of how your business is doing. Failing to understand your numbers is essentially setting yourself up for failure. As a business owner, you are responsible for the finances of your business. As a director, it is your job to develop a level of understanding of the finances and its performance. Being on top of the business' finances will help keep your stress levels down, and help you make the right decisions, fast.

Look regularly at inventory and see if there are ways to improve your cashflow. Keep receivables as low as possible. Reserve regularly for quarterly or annual tax returns, so there will be no surprises which can kill your cash level. If you don't manage your money, the lack of it will manage you!

Don't neglect your customers or your employees, thinking they will stay with you for ever! Stay regularly in contact with customers, asking if they are content with product quality and the service level you are offering.

Take time to regularly evaluate not only your employee's performance but also your own as a manager! Ask them how you are doing as their manager. One of my leaders always used to say, delegation is good, but control is better! Don't delegate too much until you know and have experienced that the employee is trustworthy and will do the job as you would!

Biblical wisdom for a farming business can be found in Proverbs 27:23-27. "Be sure you know the condition of your flocks, give careful attention to your herds; for riches do not endure forever, and a crown is not secure for all generations. When the hay is removed, and new growth appears and the grass from the hills is gathered in, the lambs will provide you with clothing, and the goats with the price of a field. You will have plenty of goats' milk to feed your family and to nourish your female servants."

Of course, this is also good advice for a regular business today! Know the condition of the business, give careful attention to it, remembering that the economy changes, customers get new needs, employees leave and you may lose a prominent role in your market.

THE DONKEY AT WORK

The Donkey at Work

The donkey at work says, "Here I am! Please use me to help others!"

To love your neighbor as yourself will be one of the more important results of tying your donkey to the vine. Jesus told the story of the Good Samaritan who, on his way from Jerusalem to Jericho, found a beaten and robbed Jew alongside the road to illustrate this principle. The Samaritan traveler was merciful and looked after the wounded Jewish man: "A Samaritan, as he traveled, came where the man was; and when he saw him, he took pity on him. He went to him and bandaged his wounds, pouring on oil and wine. Then he put the man on his own donkey, took him to an inn and took care of him. The next day he took out two silver coins and gave them to the innkeeper. "Look after him," he said, "and when I return, I will reimburse you for any extra expense you may have." (Luke 10:33–35). Mercy in action!

Blessed are the Merciful!

To the Samaritan, this was an opportunity to love his neighbor and use his assets to show compassion and mercy to someone in need. The London Times some years ago publicized the results of an investigation among young professionals that showed that two-thirds of those ambitious and affluent people felt no responsibility whatsoever to help anybody worse off than themselves!

How can we use our donkeys and look after the poor among us? Here are some examples.

- Recently I heard of a Dutch businessman who took an Iranian asylum seeker into his home.

- A company made a goal to hire 10 percent of its workforce from people with a handicap.

- Another enterprise financially sponsors children from developing countries and encourages their personnel to do the same.

- Six local enterprises are employing ex-offenders, in consultation with the nearby prison.

It is a big challenge for us as Christian entrepreneurs to give a new dimension to the idea of stewardship. We have to learn what it means to use part of the assets of the company in a non-economical way, just like the Good Samaritan did when he used his donkey to help his neighbor. After all, it cost him time and money. In another scenario, Jesus praised the shrewd manager because he forgave his debtors up to half of their debt. He said, "Here's the lesson: Use your worldly resources to benefit others and make friends. Then, when your earthly possessions are gone, they will welcome you to an eternal home" (Luke 16:9 nlt).

The golden rule in the Bible is "Do to others whatever you would like them to do to you. This is the essence of all that is taught in the law and the prophets" (Matt. 7:12 nlt). This stands in contrast to the prevailing rule of our culture, which tells us, "He who has the gold rules!"

I remember the head of a sales department at Samsonite having this biblical golden rule engraved on a coin and giving it to his sales force. Every time they had a tough time negotiating, they asked the question, "If you were in my shoes, what would you think to be an honest deal? How would you like me to treat you?" Now that is what we call living together, hearts meeting hearts. This is an action that brings people together toward a common goal in a manner profitable to both parties—a win-win situation!

A Donkey collapsing under his load

One of the tenets of the Old Testament Jewish law was "If you see that the donkey of someone who hates you has collapsed under its load, do not walk by. Instead, stop and help" (Exodus 23:5).

When a problem in the business of a colleague is brought to your attention, it could be God's invitation for you to become significant in the life of this person.

I once had a serious discussion with the credit controller of our company. When dealing with a client who didn't pay his invoices on time, he acted like a terrier—he sank his teeth in and wouldn't let go. In fact he earned his money by keeping the receivables position on a healthy level of about thirty days. That day he had already lost his patience to a salesman of our products. This guy was an independent sales rep for a range of chemicals for the meat processing industry, and one of the best in his trade. He knew the industry and the needs of the clients very well, but his administration was, just like with so many good salespeople, very chaotic, and that is why he constantly owed us money. The credit controller wanted to send the collection agency to his home. I knew this would probably mean the end of our relationship. I asked for one more chance for him and promised to go see the salesman immediately.

That same day I went to visit him at home, which was also his office. I stepped into his office and nearly fell over the piles of paper and files on the floor. He did not have a filing system, but a 'piling system!' While we talked over a cup of coffee, I learned that he too was at his wit's end and did not know how to look after his administration. After a few more discussions, we decided to take over his one-man business and bring him on board to work for us, so that in future we could issue the invoices and collect them on time. He was very grateful to us for looking a bit further than the cold figures and wanting to meet him as a person. In his eyes this was a testimony of love of one's neighbor, and being a Christian clearly rose in his esteem. He became a top salesman! Be aware of business associates who are in difficulties. You will find many opportunities to witness in word and deed about the love of God!

Helping to carry the Load

Jesus said of the religious leaders of his day, "They tie up heavy loads and put them on men's shoulders, but they themselves are not willing to lift a finger to move them" (Matt. 23:4). Heavy loads—like shiploads, or containers. That is the meaning of the Greek words 'barea fortia' used here. Heavy loads, too heavy to lift!

Jesus spoke here about the burden of laws and regulations. We could add unspoken expectations. Our task as leader of the organization is to unburden co-workers and free them to serve God as he has gifted and directed them. We need to serve instead of rule. As followers of Jesus, we should offer them the same words Jesus said: "Come to me, all you who are weary and burdened, and I will give you rest" (Matt. 11:28). To help carry burdens gives us an excellent chance to be Christlike to our people. In difficult times of loss and inability we can show mercy and love.

Do not Form an Unequal Yoke

To an entrepreneur, deciding whether to enter into a business partnership is a major and important decision. I find it striking that the Bible strongly advises against it. In the Old Testament we read, "You must not plow with an ox and a donkey harnessed together" (Deut. 22:10 nlt).

A practical reason for this is that the load on the shoulders of both animals is not equally distributed. The Bible uses an image of the yoke that is placed on the neck of the animals to assist them in carrying out their heavy work. If the two animals in the yoke are not equally matched in size and strength, then an excessive burden is placed on one, and that animal could easily break its neck.

Another practical reason is infertility. When a donkey and a horse have a colt together, we call it a mule. Although a mule can carry huge loads, it is sterile and cannot conceive and bring forth young. Unequally-yoked business partners will not be able to bear fruit in their business dealings because of their differing values.

Paul mentions a spiritual reason in 2 Corinthians 6:14–15. "Do not be yoked together with unbelievers. For what do righteousness and wickedness have in common? Or what fellowship can light have with darkness? What harmony is there between Christ and Belial? What does a believer have in common with an unbeliever?"

Ultimately in a conflict with a partner, the Christian will have to compromise his faith and values, bringing disastrous consequences for the Christian entrepreneur himself and causing the work of God through the company to be hindered. In the Bible we read of an example of a terrible alliance between successful King Jehoshaphat and godless King Ahaziah. "Jehoshaphat king of Judah made an alliance with Ahaziah king of Israel, who was guilty of wickedness. He agreed with him to construct a fleet of trading ships. After these were built at Ezion Geber, Eliezer son of Dodavahu of Mareshah prophesied against Jehoshaphat, saying, "Because you have made an alliance with Ahaziah, the Lord will destroy what you have made." The ships were wrecked and were not able to set sail to trade." (2 Chron. 20:35–37).

Jehoshaphat had not learned a thing from his former alliance with Ahab (2 Chron. 18:18–34) or from his father's failed alliance with Aram (2 Chron. 16:2–9).

These partnerships were examples of an unequal yoke, because the one served the Lord wholeheartedly, while the other clearly had different priorities that did not include the Lord.

Before entering into a partnership, ask yourself the following questions:

- What are my motives?

- What problems am I endeavoring to avoid in this way?

- Is this partnership the best solution, or is it only a quick solution?

- Did I pray about it and ask other people's advice?

- Do my partner and I want to achieve the same goals?

- Am I willing to do what God asks of me with less financial gain?

Matthew, in his report on Jesus' entry into Jerusalem, used the Greek word 'hupozugion,' literally meaning "one under a yoke" to describe the donkey Jesus rode on. That is the best "yoke" for us as Christian entrepreneurs to be under—in partnership with Jesus in our business!

Never on a Sunday

In Old Testament times donkeys had to rest on the Sabbath.

"Observe the Sabbath day by keeping it holy, as the Lord your God has commanded you. Six days you shall labor and do all your work, but the seventh day is a Sabbath to the Lord your God. On it you shall not do any work, neither you, nor your son or daughter, nor your manservant or maidservant, nor your ox, your donkey or any of your animals, nor the alien within your gates, so that your manservant and maidservant may rest, as you do. Remember that you were slaves in Egypt and that the Lord your God brought you out of there with a mighty hand and an outstretched arm. Therefore the Lord your God has commanded you to observe the Sabbath day." (Deut. 5:12–15)

A key task for a Christian entrepreneur is to take time to get enough rest, reflection, and recreation, not only for himself but also for his employees. The reason for honoring the Sabbath, as stated in this verse, is that God delivered us from slavery with his mighty hand and outstretched arm! A day of rest is a celebration; in fact it is a holiday.

During my whole career I always made it a habit never to work on a Sunday. There will always be problems to solve, deadlines to reach, offers to prepare. Consciously resting on a Sunday is a demonstration of dependence on God. It is taking a conscious step to approach God, trusting that he will take care of all things. Too often entrepreneurs find themselves on a Sunday morning already concerned about their Monday morning problems. Jesus said, "But seek first his kingdom and his righteousness, and all these things will be given to you as well. Therefore do not worry about tomorrow, for tomorrow will worry about itself. Each day has enough trouble of its own" (Matt. 6:33–34).

Gary Grant calls himself "The Entertainer." He is managing director and founder of this chain of stores across the UK. The chain of stores is called "The Entertainer". And is UK's largest independent toy retailer, operating 149 stores with revenues of over GBP 140 million, employing up to 2000 people, depending om the season. Gary Grant left school with one O-level, in maths, and opened his first toy shop at the age of 23. He had been sacked from his job in a bike shop and with his wife, Cath, managed to borrow enough money to buy a failing toy shop in Amersham.

Gary found Christ after being invited to a men's breakfast at his local church on a Saturday. Nothing specific happened, but "it all fell into place". By the end of that weekend, his life was "turned completely upside down". He describes himself as a "charismatic evangelical" and admits his business is run on Biblical principles. "You cannot be a Christian on Sundays without this filtering through to the week ahead. Faith is a living, daily thing. Considering 'What does God want me to do?' is as important Monday to Friday as on a Sunday."

Looking back to when he became a Christian at 33, Gary says, "Why didn't somebody tell me about Jesus earlier?'"

Gary will not allow his stores to open on Sundays because of his faith. He said: "We don't trade on Sundays, any Sundays of the year, and as Christmas Eve 2017 falls on a Sunday, we will be closed for what will be the second largest trading day of the year. As a Christian, I believe in families. And just being around for our children and our grandchildren, being able to have one day that we can meet together, we can eat together and stay together as a family, I think is very important. I know that if I do what I do with the right motive with the right intention, that I can rely on the fact that God will honour that."

In 1995, when Sunday trading became legal, God challenged me: "Are you going to give up Sunday trading? Keeping the Sabbath holy is one of the 10 commandments, so I felt that I shouldn't be opening the doors on a Sunday. For many of our 1,700 staff, they say that the fact that they can have a day off with the family on a Sunday is really important to them, regardless of what they believe." Mr Grant estimated his stores could take around 1.5 percent of their annual turnover if they opened on Christmas Eve.

He said: "I wrestled with this concept of Sundays. I really felt the Lord was saying to me, "Gary – just be closed on a Sunday"."

Mr Grant said: "People have said "What, even with Christmas Eve being a Sunday, you're closed?" And I say "Well, what's the difference? The principle is a day of rest. A good number of the staff, from now until Christmas, may well be working six days a week, and long days. They have given their all, and they need a break. And on a seven day cycle, that's what Sundays are.

This business will never open on a Sunday whilst I'm a shareholder.... If this business ever needs for its survival to trade on a Sunday, it's up for sale."

Care

On what is now known as Palm Sunday, Jesus rode a young donkey into Jerusalem. I am writing this at the beginning of what we call the Passion Week, which is the week when Jesus showed us the most important aspect of his character: love. His passion, his love, compelled him to make the greatest sacrifice: laying down his life for his friends.

I recently heard an acquaintance ask, "Why do I not care so much about my co-workers and clients anymore?" One of the biggest problems in our relationships with others is the emotional energy it costs to show kindness and affection for our employees. The reason could be that we're just too tired, the so-called "compassion fatigue," an expression created by researchers, and a cousin of burnout. It means you feel too tired to care for anybody. You have nothing left to give. You are not willing to help others anymore.

Direct research (Academy of Management Review, 18:621–36) points to these five most important causes of compassion fatigue:

1. Too many hours in the office, called "quantitative role overload"

2. Working for an unpleasant boss

3. Doing work you are not really qualified for

4. Doing work that demands that you deal with the problems of others

5. A discrepancy between your values and those of your employer

According to this research, the results of this emotional drain are as follows:

- A withdrawal from the people around you

- Less time spent in the presence of others

- Less tolerance towards people who act difficult to at times

- Experience of moodiness and impatience

- Less compassion

- Indifference

Jesus clearly showed compassion and love for people. Matthew 9:36 says, "When he saw the crowds, he had compassion on them, because they were harassed and helpless, like sheep without a shepherd."

The acronym CARE gives some tips on caring for our employees:

- Challenge your employee to grow spiritually. A good boss knows the importance of turning the conversation toward matters of faith at the appropriate time.

- Affirm your employees' value. A phone call or a note can let your employee know how important he or she is and can keep your relationship strong.

- Respect the feelings and wishes of your employees. No one wants a boss with whom ideas, dreams, and concerns fall on deaf ears. A good boss is a great sounding board.

- Encourage your employees with compliments and by doing good deeds. Your employees will feel better after having been in your presence.

The wise saying is so true. "People don't care how much you know, until they know how much you care!"

"Everything You've Heard so Far is Not True"

Imagine the end of a day's sales conference at a large insurance company. The invited keynote speaker gets up and delivers this bombshell: "Everything you've heard so far is not true." Tony Campolo, then professor emeritus of sociology at Eastern University in Pennsylvania, opened his speech with this statement after some power speakers had instructed the audience on how to "set up" clients, push the right emotional buttons, and close the deal. Tony's task was to "psych up" the audience for a last big motivational push. You can imagine the shock when he said, "Everything you've heard so far is not true!"

"People are not things to be manipulated with the right techniques," he said, "not economic objects. They are entitled to love." The audience was enthralled as he made a case to make "love" a verb demonstrated daily in the office and the factory. An article in the magazine, Fast Company, had a great title; "Love: The Killer App!" In the leader, Yahoo senior executive Tim Sanders wrote, "The most powerful force in business isn't greed, fear, or even the raw energy of unbridled competition. The most powerful force in business is love." He gives a powerful definition. Love "is the selfless promotion of the growth of the other."

Loving people never comes easy. We tend to be selfish and greedy instead of seeking the best for the other, so how do we tap into the source? "He will tether his donkey to a vine, his colt to the choicest branch" (Genesis 49:11). These words given by patriarch Jacob to his fourth son, Judah, give the secret to an unending flow of love. Park your donkey (your business, assets, career, assignment) alongside the true Vine, which is Jesus himself, and experience how the life of the Vine flows through the branches and into the donkey, and bears fruit—the greatest of which is love.

Tony Campolo described love at work in a very practical paraphrase of 1 Corinthians 13:

"Although I have the communication skills of men and angels and have not love, I sound just like a clanging cymbal. If I can predict business trends and have a total grasp of the latest production techniques, and have the kind of positive thinking that people say is the secret of success but have no love, it really does no lasting good. And although I make all the sacrifices so that there can be better wages for my workers, and make sure they have all the fringe benefits possible and do not show them love, it will still leave them grumbling and discontented. Love teaches me to put up with a lot of things that would ordinarily make me angry, and it makes me into a listening, sensitive person. It keeps me from acting like a big shot and going on ego trips. Love keeps me from being rude to even the lowliest person in the company. It keeps me from demanding that things al- ways be done my way; it keeps me from blowing up at the least little thing. And it prevents me from keeping files on all the mistakes made by people working for me. Love gets no satisfaction out of the failures of others—even when their failures guarantee that I will get a promotion."

Want a new source of assets to invest in your company? Tie your donkey to the Vine and let the dynamic life of Jesus flow through giving you energy and power to love!

LESSONS FROM LIFE AND LEADERS

10

This book is all about the prophecy of arch father Jacob to his fourth son, Judah. 'He shall tether his donkey to a vine.' In the words preceding this, Jacob sketched the role Judah would play in Israel. He was to be a leader.

I remember a wonderful advertisement by Budweiser beer, which was shown during the interval at the Super Bowl game. It showed the six huge, powerful Clydesdale horses as they proudly pulled a large carriage of beer barrels. They were beautifully groomed, including the white mane and the long white hairs around the lower part of their legs. The next shot was of a donkey with big dreams - of becoming a Clydesdale! The only problem was. - he was a little donkey. The ad showed the donkey practicing the Clydesdale walk, pulling the heavy carriage and even using white, flowing hair extensions on his neck and around his legs! Eventually, he went for his big job interview and stood before a row of six huge Clydesdales. "What makes you think you could become a Clydesdale, son?" asked one of the horses. The donkey looked the giant horses straight in the eye, and exclaimed loudly, with mouth wide open and teeth bared, "Ee-yy-ooorrre." He got the job and was placed right at the front of the team, proudly leading the other horses pulling the carriage!

A wonderful example of being called as a leader.

Jacob's assignment for Judah was as follows. "Judah, your brothers will praise you; your hand will be on the neck of your enemies; your father's sons will bow down to you. You are a lion's cub, Judah; you return from the prey, my son. Like a lion he crouches and lies down, like a lioness—who dares to rouse him? The scepter will not depart from Judah, nor the ruler's staff from between his feet, until he to whom it belongs shall come and the obedience of the nations shall be his."

Judah was to lead his family through personal trials, failures and tough times. He was to be as fearless as a lion and take up the role of a ruler, a leader, until The One came to whom true leadership belongs - Jesus Himself!

I believe that tying your donkey to the Vine, will make you become a leader in your family, business, community and the wider world. A leader is a learner and I would like to look back on how I was shaped as a leader.

Socrates said, "The unexamined life is not worth living." I will now take you on a short journey through the past decades of my life, examining what I have learned about life and leadership. I hope we can all learn lessons from the past. George Santanyana stated, "Those who cannot remember the past are condemned to repeat it."

50-ies

I was born at an early age, in 1950 in the fishing port of Fleetwood on the north west coast of England. My recollections of my early days were of freedom and fun. My mother ran a small guest house on the sea front together with my grandfather who was living with us. My father was a site accountant for a firm of civil engineers and he was away from home for long periods at various construction sites in the north of England. I spent my days on the beach, fishing for shellfish and crabs under the lifeboat slipway which was totally forbidden! I was learning that leadership needs a strong sense of adventure!

I think that my grandfather was my most influential leader during the 50-ies. He was a man of principle, a teetotaler, a Methodist – and he spent time with me. Richard Leider wrote in his book on leadership, "the greatest challenge of a leader is to lead yourself." Without self-discipline, a leader can never be effective. Grandpa Taylor was very disciplined and willingly adhered to the self-constraints of the Methodist faith in Christ.

My fondest memories of this decade concern travel. Travelling with my grandfather to football matches and for holidays. I learned from him that a leader must spend time with those he is leading. There is no substitute for proximity. A focus of the strategy of Jesus Himself was, to "choose twelve, that they may be with Him."

Europe was recovering from the trauma of World War 2 and starting to enjoy some affluence. During this decade, the first steps towards European integration were taken by the Schumann plan initiating the European Coal and Steel Community, which later developed into the European Economic Community. The architect was the Frenchman Jean Monnet, whose leadership in achieving this remarkable feat was described, "he asked for no authority over anyone, but showed remarkable people skills and consensus building, motivated by his catholic convictions on love, solidarity and justice" – essential leadership skills today.

He was supported by another of my 'leadership heroes', the German chancellor Konrad Adenauer, who led Germany out of destruction into the well-publicized "Wirtschaftswunder" of amazing economic growth, leaving we Brits wondering who had really won the war! When Billy Graham asked him, "Mr. Chancellor, do you believe in Jesus?", Adenauer replied, "Young man, without Christ, we have no hope!"

60-ies

My father was moving around the country for his work and we moved house several times during the next few years like hermit crabs. This had a profound effect on me as a young boy. Finding it impossible to keep friends for long, I started to doubt myself and to develop a kind of inferiority complex. I began then to ask myself questions like;

Who am I? Why am I here? What is life all about? My grandfather passed away in the early 60-ies, and I missed that great leader.

Another leader to pass away in the early 60-ies was my hero, Winston Churchill. If ever a man had failed during his long career, it was he. From him I learned that it does not matter how many times you fall, but that you get up one more time. He warned about the diabolical division of Europe which was to reach a climax in 1961 with the overnight appearance of the Berlin Wall. No-one would listen. I learned that a leader with vision is not always understood, or that people may not want to see the consequences of what will happen. His ability as a leader was a readiness to stand resolute but alone on a principle and do what is right.

Churchill was a brilliant politician, but not very good at dealing with women. One of his main opponents in the Commons was the first woman to be a minister, Lady Astor. She got very cross with Sir Winston during one debate. "Sir Winston! If you were my husband, I would put arsenic in your tea!" Winston replied, "Lady Astor, if I was your husband, I would gladly drink it!"

The move to unity in Europe was thwarted. The Soviet Union prevented impoverished citizens of a failed system from pouring en-masse into a thriving one. An example of bad leadership, Khrushchev, Brezhnev & Co. seeking to lead through repression and terror, building a society which could never last.

The next leader to have an influence on my life was the captain of our school rugby team, Graham Nutter. I was a big lad, a bit overweight, but I loved sports, especially soccer and rugby. Graham was small, but really fast, an ideal scrum half. He befriended me and encouraged and stimulated me to maintain the high British ideals of 'fair play', 'team spirit' and 'never give up'. He helped me to develop a winning mentality, to outwit the competition and go for gold. I learned from him that effective leaders have a vision of winning, reaching the goal, but playing fair and being, as we Brits say, a jolly good sport.'

He was also a Christian. Although I was brought up as a child in the Methodist church, I had stopped attending, thinking it totally irrelevant to my passion which was football!

Graham was an active member of the local Church of England which had an active sports program. I was invited to play in a national 7 a-side soccer competition, in which we reached the semi-finals and had a great day. At the end of the day, there was a speech by an evangelist who explained what a Christian really is.

He explained that God wanted me and loved me, and that he had a great plan for my life. The problem was, however, that I had turned my back on Him and he could not communicate with me. I had lost any chance of a relationship with Him, the reason for my life! I was spiritually dead – that was certainly true. I had no clue about spiritual reality! That was why God came to me, in the form of Jesus, a man with whom I could relate. I was told that Jesus had died on a cross, which I knew, but that he rose again from the dead. Having gone through death Himself, He could take me through death also, to live forever with him.

It was explained that Jesus was knocking at the door of my heart, and that if I heard his voice and opened the door, he would come in and start a loving relationship with me.

I really wanted that – to know this Jesus who loved me so much! That night, I asked Him to forgive me and to come into my life and I found a friend for life. I became a Christian at the age of 16.

Europe was facing years of troubling uncertainty under the threat of invasion and nuclear war. Proof that the East was well and truly under lock and key, came in 1968, when the Soviets invaded Prague, ousting the government of Alexander Dubcek. The cold war ended abruptly with what was called 'the Prague Spring." He was an example of a leader standing up for what is right and defying authority. That was a defining theme for the second half of the sixties. Our struggle with authority was great, fueled by riots in universities like the Sorbonne, following the example of their American counterparts at institutions like Berkeley.

This struggle reached my alma mater at a provincial English university of technology where I studied chemistry and management.

I, together with millions of 'baby boomers' were reacting against all authority – of our parents, our professors, the government – all of whom, we believed, had made a mess of our society. This was enhanced by the emergence of a global pop culture, which was naively idealistic and astoundingly hedonistic. The Beatles from Liverpool, Mary Quant's mini's down the streets of Chelsea, the sexual freedom expressed in the musical Hair, experiencing ecstasy with LSD, the opening of mystic minds through the Maharishi's meditations… all these were powerful cultural leaders for young men like me.

This clashed, of course, with my commitment to God as a follower of Jesus. I had trouble with distinguishing who George Harrison's "My Sweet Lord' really was. The dawning of the age of Aquarius, the new age had begun.

A student friend said at the time, "Marx is dead, God is dead, and I don't feel very well myself!"

I learned from this time that a leader must know and understand the culture in which he is living and the currents which force people down a certain path through constantly changing waters. I realized we, as leaders, must help people find Simon and Garfunkel's fixed, unchangeable "Bridge over Troubled Waters."

It was also a time of increasing prosperity, but we had this nagging feeling that materialism would just not yield those fruits we needed to satisfy our spiritual searching.

A leader at that time was Robb Powrie Smith, who lead a student movement called The Navigators at my univerity. His home was open to students who came in for coffee and a chat about Christian life. He helped me to understand the Bible, teaching us to study and even memorize portions which would enrich our souls and help us to make decisions which were beneficial to our lives. I learned from him the value of allowing people just to look into a happy, balanced marriage, to observe how they related to one another and their children. He said to me, "If it does not work at home, don't export it!" A long-lasting lesson for me as a leader!

This was a lesson I still had to learn – the hard way!

70-ies

At the beginning of the 70-ies, I spent a year in Holland working at the Unilever laboratory in Rotterdam, where I met my wife, Didie. I have been blessed by a wife who is older and wiser than I. Forming a marriage team, it is important that I as a leader must learn to learn from her, and in certain areas be willing to follow. A good leader must be a good follower!

Marriage is one of the most crucial areas for personal growth and we were about to learn some crucial lessons as we built our marriage together.

Europe's years of prosperity and economic growth came to an abrupt halt in 1973 after the Middle east War, and the ensuing Arab embargo on oil, which triggered huge inflation and plunged Europe into recession.

I had just started off on my business career with Brent Chemicals International in London. We were specialized in chemicals for the aerospace and engineering industries. I remember a big leadership lesson from my first boss, Bill Cross who was a Christian businessman. I knew him from the youth group through which I had become a Christian and fancied my chances as a 'protégé', an upcoming young executive. My first 6 months was to be spent as a travelling salesman, selling degreasers to garages – not exactly what I had in mind for a brilliant business career. I had no drivers license and had to travel on the underground and busses with a huge case of samples. I expected a status, I got a lesson in selling to tough people. Starting at the bottom is good for those who are leading. Bill said, "if you are going to lead salesman, you must know what it is like to sell. If you haven't done it yourself, you can never lead others in doing it."

If the 60-ies challenged authority, the 70-ies challenged competence. OPEC challenged our ability to run an economy, the report of the Club of Rome, challenged our competence to conserve our environment and the Cold War and other troubles like those in Northern Ireland challenged our political competence. Credibility of leadership was to decline sharply after this.

My company gave me the opportunity in 1974 to move to Holland to open a sales office. We expanded the business into the still lucrative nuclear engineering field and acquired a small company serving the food industries. I was appointed managing director, one of my goals achieved before I was 30. I was climbing the ladder of success. However, I had never learned to integrate my Christian faith into my business life. They were two entirely separate areas. I was a Christian on Sundays but the next day, it was business as usual, following not Gods laws but the laws of the market.

I achieved career success, but at a price. Succeeding in business while losing your soul. I was rapidly losing my relationship with God, and my marriage was at breaking point. Stress was breaking me up internally and I started to make some really bad decisions. Moreover, I was not communicating with anybody about this, not wanting to be accountable to anyone.

Consequently, the company was frauded by our accountant, we lost some major clients due to bad service, I got a slipped disk hauling heavy chemical drums about, and totally neglected my wife and children at that time.

Climbing the ladder of success, I discovered that my ladder was leaning against the wrong wall!

The Bible says, "What will it profit a man if he gains the whole world but loses his soul?" I started to listen again. First of all to God, then my wife and then to some friends, who helped me sort out my life again.

A leadership lesson learned here is that a leader must be a good listener and be willing to receive advice and guidance. I was pursuing my career, not willing to listen to warnings or good advice. Fatal for a leader!

80-ies

A key leader in the 80-ies was, of course, Mikhael Gorbachov of whom the other strong leader of the eighties, the Iron lady Margaret Thatcher said, "At least we men can do business together!" She certainly had no time for wimps and did not shirk tough decisions as a leader.

Gorbachov realized that in the Soviet Union, outputs were falling and there was no way to increase inputs. I learned from one of my mentors during this time, "if your output exceeds your input, then the upkeep will be your downfall." Gorbachov certainly realized this. He thought first that he could reinvigorate society, to rejuvenate the economy with a new openness 'glasnost'. He soon concluded that a basic restructuring was necessary a 'perestroika.' Sometimes, a leader must realise if something can be reinvigorated with adjustments or a fresh injection of enthusiasm, or if it must be completely re-built. It has been said that God is not in the business of adjusting people but renewing them, and that means starting from scratch! Gorbachov was smart enough to realise this.

And so, we came to the momentous turn in 1989, a geo-political upheaval which caught all Europe's leaders asleep. It seemed to have happened overnight.

A leader like Lech Walensa, a very courageous Catholic Union leader, showed us how to stand up for justice and freedom, deciding it was time to confront the mammoth, overwhelming communist system. In 1981, the Red Army maneuvered on Poland's eastern border, evident that Brezhnev would deploy his tank divisions. In answer to the Soviet taunt of 'how many divisions does the Pope have?' – John Paul II, said that should the Soviet tanks move, he would return to stand alongside his countrymen.

During the early 80-ies, I joined up with some men from CBMC, (Christian Business Man's Committees), who taught me to integrate my faith into my business life. My leader at this time was an Amsterdam banker called Lieko Helmus, who influenced me in this area. I first observed a leader who strove to apply Christian principles in the rough and tumble financial markets. If a leader is not a man of integrity, that is when his walk matches his talk in all areas of life, then he will quickly lose followers. With Lieko Helmus, I saw a leader who was first of all a Christian and then someone who applied his Christian faith at the bank, in his relationship with his colleagues and, of course, at home.

A leader who further influenced my future career during the 80-ies, was Albert Diepeveen, a Dutch émigré to the US. He returned to Holland at the beginning of the eighties as a man on a mission. He had found a new relationship with Jesus in the US, experiencing God at work in his family and business, and wanted intensely to help his fellow countrymen to experience this also. He challenged local Dutch CBMC leaders to get serious with their faith, because here was a great country in dire spiritual need. A leadership crisis was taking place in Holland, illustrated by the Queen's husband being involved in taking bribes from Lockheed officials for the sale of planes to the military. Diepeveen put many hours and dollars into giving CBMC a new start with a new vision. I took up this challenge and started to give first one day and then two days a week to developing this work of CBMC to meet needs of business and professional people in Holland.

Without a clear vision and the will to see it through until it becomes reality a leader is ineffective. Diepeveen was an example to me in the area of giving. Giving up a well-paid career for an economically uncertain future, was no big deal, because as Albert always says, "you cannot out-give God."

A leader must love, and to love is to give, otherwise it leads to manipulation. Diepeveen incorporates these traits.

At the end of the eighties, I was challenged by one of my friends, the hotelier Ger Cok in Amsterdam. He saw a need to reach business people for Christ in other parts of Europe. He gave a vision for me and a promise from the prayer of Jabez. "Jabez cried out to the God of Israel, 'Oh, that you would bless me and enlarge my territory! Let your hand be with me, and keep me from harm so that I will be free from pain.' And God granted his request." (1 Chronicles 4:10). God certainly answered this request. Within 4 months, the Berlin Wall collapsed, opening up all of Eastern Europe for the gospel. To date, the ministry I started has been active in about 35 nations and God has faithfully provided all we needed.

90-ies

In the surge toward freedom, it took Poland 10 years, Hungary 10 months, East Germany 10 weeks, Czechoslovakia 10 days and Romania 10 hours – but it still took everyone in Europe by surprise. Out of a Europe of less than 20 nations, arose a new Europe of more than 45 nations within a couple of years.

The 12 members of the European Community pledged to create one market, the world's largest by December 31, 1992. Europe's next transformation would be politically from community to a full Union.

This trend and countertrend have dominated Europe during the 90-ies. On the one hand, a unity motivated by economic and political pragmatism. At the very least, one commentator has said, it has all been worth it, because we have not been at war since 1945! On the other hand, social and cultural needs have created new boundaries as 'tribes' and new nations confirm their presence as separate entities. Basques, Scots, Catalans, Croats, Serbs, the Lombards of northern Italy are just a few examples of the struggle for independence and the assurance of maintaining cultural identity and uniqueness.

I was impressed that this all had a place in God's ultimate purpose and plan for Europe. The apostle Paul wrote to the Athenians, who were experiencing the decline of Greece, " He (God) determined the exact time set for them and the exact places where they should live. God did this so that men would seek him and perhaps reach out for him and find him, though he is not far from each one of us."

God's leadership during all of this was evident to me. History is His-story, and he unfolds it before our eyes for a purpose. As Einstein said, "God does nor play dice with the world."

I started the organization called Europartners to present Christ as Saviour and Lord to business and professional leaders all over Europe. I travelled extensively throughout Eastern Europe and the former Soviet Union and was amazed at the degree of hunger and thirst for spiritual truth and the search for God in nations which had denied the existence of God. It reinforced the statement of the 17th. Century French mathematician Pascal, the father of modern computing, "In every man there is a God-shaped void which only He can fill." People were embracing Jesus of Nazareth and rediscovering eternal truth.

I also met leaders who had come through the communist experiment, through severe repression, torture and imprisonment, emerging unscathed in their integrity. Leaders such as pastor Jozef Bondarenko, imprisoned for many years, inhumanly treated at the hands of his Soviet tormentors, such as having to lie down in a flooded cell in the freezing cold, allowing a fellow inmate to sleep dry on top of him. Such as Hungarian leader, Prof. Jenö Barátossy who was re-instated in the early 90-ies as special advisor to the president after years of relegation to third class citizenship. My friends, almost all of the "heroes" who came out on top after the revolution were followers of Jesus!

I learned a lot from a Swiss lawyer, Dr. Adolf Guggenbühl, who was leader of the non-denominational Swiss association of Christian business people. They practiced a policy, which was originally coined by St. Augustine. "In essentials unity, in secondary matters freedom and in all things love." This gave me a love for unity in matters pertaining to salvation, where we can meet fellow believers fairly easily; freedom to worship in different forms; but in any case, practising love. Dr. Guggenbühl was an example on setting priorities, an essential skill for leaders. I remember him saying that your priorities have little to do with how much time spent. If it did, sleeping would be number one! Your priorities should determine choices; in any conflicting situation, your priorities detemine what choice to make.

My closest personal example of leadership comes from the Chairman of CBMC in Europe, Jim Johnston from Belfast, Northern Ireland. Next to the inherent Irish capacity for humor, he has a knack of saying the right thing at the right time. This defuses tense situations between people, a skill he has learned in the political turmoil of Northern Ireland. Humour and timing are two essential traits of a leader. I will say no more about him. As he wisely once replied to someone asking him why he said so little, "it's better for people to wonder why you didn't say anything than to wonder why you did!"

I learned a lot from Dr. Siegfried Buchholz, a CEO from Vienna. He taught me important principles of leadership. "If you think you are leading and no-one is following, you are just having a nice walk in the park." Followers form an acid-test of leadership. I have always been able to find someone to take over my tasks, share my vision and continue a ministry.

The Cold War ended, Nelson Mandela was released from prison, the internet changed life as everyone knew it—in many ways, the 1990s seemed a decade of both hope and relief.

00-ies

The 'noughties' decade, started with 9/11 and increasing jihadism. It has been called the decade of fear and distrust. In the 00-ies, we had a leadership vacuum – a vacuum which is sucking into it new power structures which have been emerging during the past decades. Military power such as we are seeing in Ireland, Spain, Bosnia, Chechnya. Economic power through the Mafia, coming out of its Russian base and influencing business throughout Europe. Religious power coming out of a very militant and fundamental Islamic movement for state influence. Influential commentators in Germany have predicted that in two generations, Germany will be an Islamic state, if things do not change. Social power, influenced by the drug trade, which globally, is now larger than the world turnover in oil.

Traditional leadership from the church, politicians, associations had been eroded away during the past decades, enjoying very little credit today. Leaders are also losing authority due to advances in information technology. Personal knowledge no longer gives authority, this knowledge becoming rapidly obsolete.

It was the decade of technology, of which perhaps Google and the ipod were icons. I learned to embrace technology as an 'early adapter', bringing increased productivity. I call this the i-Decade, in which everything became personal, characterized by the i-mac and the i-phone. Community suffered, amd people became more private.

It was a decade of financial troubles with an economy fueled by spiraling debt. We had the dot.com crisis and it was a decade of boom and bust. I invested quite a lot of money in the stock market - in the summer of 2001. Just before 9/11. It took me 7 years to get my money back! We had a global recession which started in 2007, by greedy financial speculation using new financial products which hardly anyone could understand.

It was during this decade that I got to know four pioneers of teaching finances from a Biblical perspective. Howard Dayton taught me that God is the owner of everything and has appointed you and I as managers of his possessions. Larry Burkett showed me how financial problems are an outside indicator of an inside spiritual condition and about the dangers of debt. Ron Blue taught how money was a tool, a test and a testimony. A tool with which to do good, a test of our faithfulness and a testimony to Gods provision and Biblical wisdom. Earl Pitts introduced me to mammon - the god behind money, which competes for our devotion.

I worked as managing director of a space services company with the objective of learning how to lead a company for Christ. A leader I learned a lot from was Kent Humphreys of the Fellowship of Companies for Christ. He was an example of how to use a business as a platform for ministry. I have mentioned some of the lessons learned in this book.

We published one of Kent's books, called 'Shepherding Horses.' This is a plea to bridge the gap between pastors and businesspeople, and for them to support, help and teach one another. They have such a lot to offer one another, but the business person often feels lonely and not understood in church, while the pastor is often rather envious of the business leader's freedom, resources and entrepreneurial spirit. It is so important that business people feel supported in church. That is not always the case, unfortunately.

10-s

In this decade, wars and terrorist attacks continue, trust in our politicians, financial leaders and churches continue to decline. We are increasingly unable to deal with seemingly unsolvable problems such as climate change, migrants, national and personal debt and poverty. We are connected to one another technologically, but not personally.

So, who will give true leadership in this age? This is becoming an increasingly difficult question to answer. With the decline of moral leadership, the increasing complexity of our affairs, together with wall to wall uncertainty about a totally unpredictable future, people are looking for leaders they can follow!

In each and every decade we have experienced change. One of the key success factors in business today is the ability to deal meaningfully with change and adapt to the changing circumstances. A leader has to embrace change, and look on it as an opportunity to serve and love others. The Bible says we should not be conformed to the patterns of this world but to be transformed by the renewal of our minds. (Romans 12:2)

I visited India a few times in this decade and one of the highlights was a visit to Gandhi's home in Delhi. I was struck by a glass showcase, containing all the possessions Gandhi had when he died. The case was very small, indeed. I learned from Gandhi that a cause to live for is more important than things to accumulate. Gandhi was a change agent. He said, "Be the change that you wish to see in the world. As human beings, our greatness lies not so much in being able to remake the world – that is the myth of the atomic age – as in being able to remake ourselves."

But how can we remake ourselves? We need to be transformed.

That is what Jesus of Nazareth came to do.

Firstly, He gives us a fixed core – a rock which does not change in the centre of our lives, weathering all storms. He has promised to give us the Spirit of God the Father who enables us to do what we can not do ourselves. No-one can pull themselves up with their own shoelaces! We all need a force outside ourselves which gives the necessary power to deal with the changes occurring all around us.

Secondly, He helps us develop loving relationships from which we receive the necessary support, advice and encouragement.

Thirdly, we do not know what the future may bring. Economic prosperity again? Disaster again? Jesus will help us develop spiritual, emotional, relational wealth, so that we can be robust and content in any economic condition.

Quo Vadis?

Czech president, Vaclav Havel, tells us, that if we have learned only one lesson from the failure of the communist experiment in which humanism, the capability of man to sort out his own problems and order a utopian society, was taken to its logical conclusion, is is this - that we have experienced the death of humanism. Although people try to find meaning and identity by reaching into their inner selves through meditation, mindfulness or religion, it is clear that they are no closer to finding the answer to the questions of 'who am I?' and 'where am I going?', from inside himself.

The story is told of two sailors becoming happily inebriated in a London pub. As they came staggering outside at closing time, they bumped into an Admiral. "Men, where do you think you're going?" "No idea, mate!", replied the jolly tars. "Do you know who I am?", said the Admiral. "Now we're in real trouble," said the sailor, "we don't know where we're going, and he doesn't know who he is!

We must go back – to the future. To the Person around whom our time revolves, Jesus of Nazareth. In this decade of global change with wall-to-wall uncertainty, He is the only leader ever to stake a claim for global leadership. He is the end of religion. He said, "I am the light of the world. Whoever follows me will never walk in darkness but will have the light of life."

A good leader is a good follower. You can do no better than to be yoked with Jesus, and to follow no-one better than Jesus.

Compass - finances God's way is a global, non-denominational movement teaching financial discipleship and generosity. The purpose is to serve churches, businesses, ministries, schools and other organisations by providing biblically-based solutions on handling money and possessions. Our vision is to see everyone, everywhere faithfully living by God's financial principles in all areas of their lives.

Global mission

Compass' mission is to help people everywhere to learn, apply and teach Gods financial and business principles. We are looking for three major outcomes.

1. To know Christ more intimately as we trust and obey Him,

2. To become free from worry, fear, stress and anxiety and then be free to serve and love the Lord and our neighbours.

3. To contribute to fulfilling the Great Commission by giving our money and other resources to fund the work of the Church.

The Compass Global Team is comprised of local leadership on 6 continents – Europe, Asia, South America, North America, Africa and the Indian sub-continent. Our continental offices serve more than 90 nations around the world.

To get in touch, please visit the Compass Global landing page **www.compass1.global**

Resources

Compass has developed a wide range of resources in a wide variety of formats, such as DVD based teaching, workshops, small group studies, e-books and online learning.

There are teaching resources for all ages, from small children through students to adults; with application to areas of life such as business, church, marriage and family.Compass is active in over 80 nations over the globe and has resources in many languages. Contact our continental offices at www.compass1.global

To see specific English language resources, please visit the US shop at **www.compass1.org** or the UK shop at **www.compassuk.org**

www.ingramcontent.com/pod-product-compliance
Lightning Source LLC
LaVergne TN
LVHW010631200726